The
Political
Imperative

The Political Imperative

An Assignment from God

Norm Mason

Jebaire Publishing
Snellville, GA

ISBN-13: 978-0-9786796-9-9
Library of Congress Control Number: 2011933747

Interior Editor: Fran Lowe
Supervising Editor: Shannon Clark
Cover Design: Jebaire Publishing
Original Design Concept: Norm Mason

Visit Jebaire's website at: www.jebairepublishing.com

Jebaire Publishing, LLC is an independent, non-denominational Christian book publisher. We are a free press and report to no outside groups. Our mission is to provide relevant Christian resources that both inspire and encourage our readers to pursue a meaningful relationship with God our Father through His son Jesus Christ.

Printed in the United States

Dedication

With love to my wife Jeanie.
Thank you for your encouragement, support and partnership.

Contents

ℭ𝔯𝔢𝔣𝔞𝔠𝔢

For I have given unto them the words which thou gavest me . . .

(John 17:8a KJV)

Many men and women have been active for a number of years in the areas of public policy, civil government, and the political process because of their concern about the direction in which our country is heading. For many people, their primary motivation has arisen out of strongly held Christian convictions on some of the key issues of the day—especially, although not exclusively, social issues. These people have been variously referred to as values voters, conservative Christians, and the religious right. These three informal groupings may not be identical in their makeup, but they are certainly interrelated and overlapping. Collectively, I call them the VCR's. I am disclosing at the outset that I classify myself as a member of all three groups.

For some years I have considered the following question in regard to the Christian community, especially in America: for those of us actively involved in the civic area, why is it that we do what we do, and other Christians don't?

I concluded that one key reason more Christians aren't politically active is that most of them don't consider being highly active in civil government essential to their Christian walk. As I thought about that, I began to study and pray for some insight. It seemed to me so right to be involved in politics, but I had to admit that I could not make the case for the answer I sought: that Christian activism was much more than just a mixture of Christian concern over social issues and a general distress over the direction in which the country is heading.

Even though those reasons are sufficient for me and many others to be doing those things which we're doing, they don't necessarily make it core for most Christians—commendable perhaps, but not core. From my research on the topic came *The Political Imperative*. When I began working on this project, I didn't have a clear idea about how it would all come out; even so, it was distinctly different than I ever expected.

This is not intended to be a book about civics from a conservative perspective, or even a conservative *Christian* perspective. This publication is designed to set forth a biblical imperative for Christian engagement in the political process in a way perhaps not previously encountered by believers.

Omitted within these pages is a duplication of the very good material on Christian political participation already available. This includes extensive discussions of social ills, such as abortion; invaluable information on America's Christian heritage, including well-documented information about the Founding Fathers, which serves to provide insight into their core vision and values; explanations of how the courts and others have twisted the issue of "separation of church and state"; and instructive information on the various duplicitous tactics intended to discourage Christian involvement.

All of these are excellent topics and very important to fully understand. Regrettably, however, far too many Christians have heard extensively about these issues, time and again, but apparently never see themselves as needing to do much more than agree with what is being said—and perhaps, vote. All of these subjects are addressed in this book to some degree, but the core topic involves setting forth a more fundamental basis for Christian political engagement.

The purpose here is to present—for those who hold the Bible as absolutely authoritative for their lives—a specifically biblical basis for Christian political engagement to be viewed as an essential requirement, an imperative, and an assignment from God with no excuses allowed. Related information unquestionably informs, encourages, and even inspires, but the Bible can compel Christians with the authority of God.

So, should all of us Christians become political activists? I hesitate to say that we should all become "activists," simply because that word invokes images of people who are operating outside the norm to the degree that some would view their behavior as almost fringe. The fact is that Christians who are significantly involved deeply in public policy and political activity are all too rare—and that is a huge problem. The replacement term for "activists" that I use, which is explained throughout the book, is the phrase "Great Commission Citizen," and my reason for doing so will become readily apparent.

I believe that this book offers a fresh approach for Bible-honoring Christians to understand their proper emphasis and role in the political process. I pray that my interpretation and applications of the Scriptures respect God's intent in this area. Please proceed prayerfully, because it is what you do when you finish reading the book that really counts.

The Political Imperative

Opening Volley

Then He shall become a sanctuary; But to both the houses of Israel, a stone to strike and a rock to stumble over, And a snare and a trap for the inhabitants of Jerusalem.

(Isa. 8:14 NASB)

Have you not even read this Scripture: The stone which the builders rejected has become the chief cornerstone.

(Mark 12:10 NKJV)

What happens when a foundational building block for God's plan becomes a stumbling block to God's people? In Mark 12:10, Jesus was referring to Himself in relation to the Jewish people of His day, especially the religious leaders. More than just a foundational building block, Jesus was, and remains, the Chief Cornerstone. But for those to whom this message was initially directed, the method and message of Jesus just didn't fit their template, and they couldn't get by that. That is, it was a stumbling block.

The same problem exists today. Even though the issue does not manifest itself in the exact same manner, the way it relates to the topic of political involvement in the Christian community is rather significant.

Here is the problem:

1. One of the foundational building blocks for God's plan is civil government.

2. The single way to ensure the proper functioning of civil government, thus fulfilling God's role and achieving His

purpose, is for Christians to be highly active in public policy, civil government, and the political process.

3. It is the role of the local church to teach and train God's people to find and fulfill God's calling for them.

4. It is a stumbling block for many Christians, ministers and laity alike, for the church to be directly involved in politics and associated activities.

5. Thus, one of the key foundational building blocks of God's plan falls into disrepair and disrepute.

6. Subsequently, Christians, as well as the cause of Christ, suffer.

What *should* we believe about the role of Christians and the church in politics? Through this book, we will sort out this matter with clarity and certainty, which is the sole purpose of all that follows. Even though right now some of us may feel that we have to watch our step regarding this topic, none of us should be stumbling over it by the time we're finished.

ONE

The Political Imperative

. . . Did you not know that I must be about My Father's business?

(Luke 2:49b NKJV)

Introduction

Christians in the United States, or any country where political freedom exists, have a strong scriptural duty to be actively engaged in civil government. Our political freedom is a God-given opportunity, relating to a God-created institution and established for a God-given purpose. As such, it must be regarded as core business in the Christian community.

This duty, or core business, forms what can properly be called a "political imperative." The call is urgent and the purpose essential. This imperative is not issued to the Christian community as a whole as some vague, general notion that "somebody needs to do something about that"; instead, it is directed to each one of us personally. As Christians, then, this is our political imperative.

As Bible-honoring Christians, we are subject to a political imperative that compels us to become "Great Commission Citizens." Both of the principles behind the political imperative and the Great

Commission citizen flow directly out of a scriptural understanding of the role and purpose of civil government, as well as for the manner and procedure that Christians should adopt when participating in the political process.

The term "political" tells *what,* the phrase "Great Commission" explains *why,* the term "citizen" describes *who,* and the term "imperative" expresses *degree.* This book explains *how.*

It is critical for Christian citizens to come to terms with the material contained herein. The role of the information within these chapters is to lay out step by step, with biblical references, the basis for the assertions made in the opening paragraphs: (1) that, as Christians, we have a political imperative; and (2) the political imperative leads us to become Great Commission citizens. Surely, if this is a biblical imperative, then we cannot ignore it; in fact, we are compelled to obey it.

By making these claims, my mission is to show those who hold a high view of the Bible as God's Word the rightful roles that the concepts of the political imperative and the Great Commission citizen play in the life of the committed Christian.

Foundations

Our political freedom is a magnificent legacy paid for with a high price throughout our national history by those in pursuit of the quest to become, and then remain, a free people. We must always be grateful for the sacrifices of the visionaries and heroes who have preceded us and made possible the freedoms we now experience.

But for us as Christians, our understanding of the ultimate source of freedom must take us one step further. Our political freedom is, in the final sense, a gift from God. Gifts from God, however, are not like the toys and games we received for our birthday or Christmas, which were just used for our pleasure and then put away or pulled out at our whim.

Indeed, the gifts from God are different; they only accrue to our benefit when used for His service. These gifts from God are actually tools that allow us to more effectively advance God's purposes.

When we do this, we are blessed; and even more important, we are given the privilege of being a blessing to others in God's name. This is true whenever we properly apply God's gifts for His purposes. Such is the case with upholding our political freedom, which should be treated just like any other area in our Christian walk.

Yet, political activity—specifically that which arises out of our Christian faith—has certainly received a mixed reception in the churches today. Some consider political activism a crucial component in the effort to counter the negative impact of the social ills that run counter to our Judeo-Christian values. Others believe that it is a worthy civic undertaking but certainly not on par with "real" church work. Still others think that political activism is outside the role of the church. Correspondingly, they may be resistive and even hostile to the subject especially in a church setting.

The following chapters, however, are designed to demonstrate with certainty that engaging in the political process should be considered a core activity in the local church and should be fully embraced and never looked down upon with disdain. The more that local churches separate themselves from the political scene, the more that church members will tend to separate their voting decisions and other political activity (if any) from their Christian values.

The indirect—and sometimes direct—message from the local church has too often been that an individual's political life and Christian walk can be divided into two separate compartments. Even though this is perhaps not an intentional message, the unspoken idea is relayed to congregations when pastors and church leaders are silent, indifferent, or resistive toward politics, especially within a church setting. This subtly antagonistic mindset is ultimately harmful to God's plan, as we shall see. On the other, hand Christian leaders would never intentionally send out messages that we can, and perhaps should, separate our family decisions from our Christian values.

It is an old but true saying that Christianity is not a religion, but a way of life regarding our relationship to Christ. As a way of life, true Christianity cannot be partitioned, or just be allowed to inform and guide one part of our lives, while bearing little or no impact on other parts of our lives. With respect to a Christian's participation in civil government, public policy, and the political process, we must understand that this should be a mainline activity—not a sideline — within one's Christian walk. Political activism should be fully embraced within the local church and never scorned by actions or attitudes formally or informally expressed by the local church leadership. And yes, it is the local church that has the God-given responsibility to teach its members these truths and then train them to apply these concepts in their lives.

One caveat to all the above should be given before we proceed any further: Our God-given, non-negotiable, biblically based, no-excuses-allowed imperative to be involved in civil government is first dependent on our God-given opportunity. Different people in their particular times and places in history were given vastly different opportunities to participate and make a meaningful contribution to the civil and political life of their day. Perhaps they dreamed about a time such as ours, but they never truly experienced it. That is true historically, and is still true today in many areas of the world.

Most Christians throughout history from the early church on have lived in circumstances where they had little or no opportunity to effectively participate in civil government. Many surely dreamed about being able to do so and would have willingly done so for the right reasons had their time and place in history availed them of the opportunity, but they never experienced such an opportunity. That desire has motivated many who come to America, from the earliest settlers until today. Those coming to America for political freedom over the last several hundred years were not the first to have such a dream – they just were blessed to have the opportunity to act on that dream.

In most regions of the world today, countries have instituted within their legal framework universal suffrage—the right of both men and women to vote. Although there may be countries where women are not allowed to vote, they are the exception to the rule. On the other hand, in many areas of the world adult citizens are allowed to vote, but because of corrupt governments the elections are just mere charades. That is, the votes don't really count in any meaningful way toward reflecting a realistic degree of political freedom. In those cases the citizens have very limited (if any) opportunities to affect the policies of their civil government.

As individuals, we are not accountable for that which we are not responsible. Yet, we are accountable for that which we are responsible. Through the political process, we are both responsible and accountable for government in the United States if we are citizens of voting age and otherwise eligible to participate in the political process.

As we think about this subject of Christian involvement in the political process, we may wisely look for a precedent within Christian history to help connect the principle to its application. For our precedent to be valid, however, we must require Christians in the example we are to study to have shared the same political opportunity that is presented to us today.

But who has had more political freedom than we have enjoyed here in the U. S.? Remember, our God-given freedom is unsurpassed. So what is the comparable precedent of Christians who have experienced the same kind of political freedom? As it turns out, we are most likely to find our best precedent for Christians experiencing political freedom in the history of the United States, so we will examine that.

Then let us, established by clear biblical principles and God-given opportunity, proceed with our study based on our unique set of conditions, along with our time and place in history. Then let us honor God's gift of political freedom by engaging in civil government, public policy, and the political process, thereby serving as a blessing and example—not only to this generation, but also to those who follow. Above all, let our actions follow a clear understanding of the Scriptures in the following chapters.

Call to Order

This book's assertion is that —supported by the Bible—as Christians, our active participation in civil government, subject to our God-given opportunity, is, in fact, an assignment from God. And if it is an assignment from God, then we certainly have been remiss about even recognizing this as such, much less following through with it. This means it's time to study, find out what this is all about and what the implications are for us individually, and then catch up on our assignment. That process becomes the initial part of coming to terms with our political imperative.

First, we will start our journey with a common point of understanding and then introduce some concepts you may not have thought about—all from the Bible. Our first point backed up by a scriptural reference is this: God created civil government. Romans 13:1 (NKJV) says, "Let every soul be subject to the governing authorities. For there is no authority except from God, and the authorities that exist are appointed by God." The word "appointed" means established or ordained. Clearly God created, established, appointed, and ordained civil government.

In the earliest verses of the Bible, we see God establishing order out of time, matter, energy, and space, which apparently had been in an unordered state (Gen. 1:2). In a similar vein, within the human social realm God created civil government to provide order out of the chaos and anarchy that would otherwise reign.

Chaos and anarchy are the antithesis of civil order and adversarial to God's plan. Thus, anarchy, and civil chaos (which ultimately leads to anarchy), stand in opposition to us as Christians. We need to be on guard against elements of anarchy and confront them when they arise.

Occasionally we read in the Old Testament about God causing confusion and disorder in the midst of those whom He opposed in order to bring about their defeat and destruction (Exod. 14:24; Josh. 10:10). God created civil government for the purpose of establishing order, and those who create anarchy through social and civil disorder impede God's work. God's civil order is a blessing, but disorder and anarchy is a curse.

The Big Three

But God did more than merely create the institution of civil government. In fact, God created three great institutions: the family, civil government, and the church. As we study the Scriptures, we notice that all of them were ordained by God and created by Christ. The authority for each of them was given to Christ *for His purposes.*

The following passage from the first chapter of the New Testament Book of Colossians explains it very well. (My commentary insertions are in brackets.)

> *And He* [Christ] *is the image of the invisible God, the first-born of all creation.* [Christ is head of the institution called the family.] *For by Him all things were created, both in the heavens and on earth, visible and invisible, whether thrones or dominions or rulers or authorities* [Christ created everything. He specifically created the institution of government and civil authority, e.g. visible thrones, dominions, rulers, and authorities.] *All things have been created by Him and for Him.* [All His creation, including government, has a role in Christ's purpose and plan.] *And He is before all things, and in Him all things hold together* [Christ is head over all the elements, and He is continuously engaged in all aspects of His creation, including government, because they continuously play a role in His purpose, as well as His plan for accomplishing that purpose.] *He is also head of the body, the church. . .* [Christ is head of the institution called the church.]
>
> *(Col. 1:15-18a NASB)*

This is the summary of the passage:

- Christ created and is the head of the institution we know as the family (v. 15).

- Christ created and is the head of the institution we know as civil government (v. 16).

- Christ created and is the head of the institution we know as the church (v. 18).

- All things were created by Him (v. 16).

- All things were created for Him to serve His purposes (v. 16).

- These three institutions were not simply ancient creations followed up by passivity and indifference on

21

the part of the Creator. But Christ is continually involved, or else these institutions would self-destruct
and not have any hope at all of ever functioning as
God designed or accomplishing His purpose (v.
17).

In addition, our Christian work is also required wherever He
is active to the degree that the individual is (1) called; (2) equipped;
and (3) given opportunity (1 Cor. 3:5-9). Of course, there is no higher
calling or privilege than to be allowed to become co-workers with
Christ to accomplish His purposes.

Christ and the Great Commission

If all things were created for Christ and to accomplish His purpose, then what was and is Christ's purpose? In Luke 19, we find
a statement in Jesus' own words that sums it up very well for our
study: "For the Son of man is come to seek and to save that which
was lost" (Luke 19:10 KJV). In pursuit of that goal, Jesus performed
a distinctive, one-time unique work, as well as established an ongoing, delegated work. For the latter He provided both a message and
a method to guide us in the work He delegated to us:

1. The distinct and unique work of Jesus was His voluntary,
    substitutionary, sacrificial, and atoning death on the
    cross, where He made provision for redemption from sin
    through His shed blood, providing salvation for all who
    accept His message and place their faith in Him alone
    for salvation. Acts 4:12 says, "And there is salvation in
    no one else; for there is no other name under heaven that
    has been given among men by which we must be saved"
    (Acts 4:12 NASB).

2. The ongoing work that Jesus established is commonly
    known as the Great Commission. Jesus gathered around
    Himself disciples, whom He taught, trained, coached,
    mentored; then He sent them (and us) out to duplicate

this practice.

In short, Jesus' mission was to establish the Great Commission (Matt. 28:18-20). He made it possible by initiating it, modeling it, and mentoring it. In His final instructions, He charged those who would be His followers to dedicate themselves to carrying it out.

And Jesus came and spoke to them, saying, 'All authority has been given to Me in heaven and on earth. Go therefore and make disciples of all the nations, baptizing them in the name of the Father and of the Son and of the Holy Spirit, teaching them to observe all things that I have commanded you; and lo, I am with you always, even to the end of the age.' Amen.
(*Matt. 28:18-20 NKJV*)

As Christians, our overriding charge from Jesus is to advance the Great Commission. In fact, all our activity should be gauged in terms of this mandate. And it is for this purpose that God ordained the creation of the family, civil government, and the church. The Bible verses we've studied indicate that truth quite clearly.

If you are a parent working to support your family and raising your children in the admonition of the Lord (Eph. 6:4 KJV), then you are doing Great Commission work. The family is one of the institutions that God ordained for Christ to accomplish His purpose. Moreover, God intended for the Christian family to be the exemplary model for the entire world to follow; therefore, it is fundamental to the Great Commission purpose of Christ.

If you are actively involved in a local New Testament church that honors and respects the Bible as God's inerrant Word; and evangelism, along with nurturing and discipling Christians in Christian growth is the bedrock of the church program, then you are engaged in Great Commission work.

If you are actively involved in the various ways available to you to help guide our government to reflect the best and highest Judeo-Christian ideals and attempting to conform the civil structure to the role and purpose that God intended, then you are engaged in Great Commission work. Jesus is there, and we should be too (Col. 1:17). Regrettably, the purpose of civil government with respect to the Great Commission is not as obvious to most Christians because it has not been a focus within the church. Thus, we will examine this issue thoroughly.

Authority and Empowerment

As we have learned from Matthew 28:18, all authority in heaven and earth has been given to Jesus. Jesus created the family, civil government, and the church, and He further legitimized each by empowering them. He has delegated authority to those who hold the responsibility for these institutions so that they can accomplish what God intends for them.

Anytime the terms "rule," "submit," "be subject to," or similar expressions in the Bible are used, they represent either the exercise of God's authority or the act of being under it.

Because the church, family, and civil government have distinctive functions, they employ very different degrees of God's delegated authority. The local church, for example, primarily exercises a very soft authority. The pastoral leadership is encouraged in the Scriptures to love, lead, nurture, guide, train, encourage, spiritually feed, counsel, exhort, and mentor. Only in the most extreme cases of transgression by its individual members is the local church body scripturally commanded to strictly discipline them.

The family, on the other hand, has a different function, so another authority structure is in place. Although the husband and wife must mutually submit to one another, the wife is scripturally charged with graciously yielding to her husband as he properly exercises the biblical headship role uniquely delegated to him. Parents have been given almost complete authority over their children within scriptural bounds, including, of course, discipline rooted in love. The primary role of the parents is meeting the physical, emotional, social, educational, and spiritual needs of their children: modeling the Christian life and walk in their own lives and fostering an environment which would nurture their children toward personally becoming Christian. Parents demonstrate their love for their children in serving the principal role in their children's maturation to adulthood, along with their walk with Christ.

Civil government focuses on those responsibilities biblically assigned to it, including the adoption of a fair-minded and impartial role with respect to its citizens, accompanied by very severe authority if necessary. Civil government can order, require, and compel, even by the power of the sword (Rom. 13:4). Within the Christian community this text from Romans has been very widely (although not universally) used to confirm God's authorization for capital punishment within the government's judicial system, as well as deadly force by police when necessary, and military action in defense of the nation.

Yes, Christ does ultimately hold all authority. Yet there is something even higher than simply holding authority and having the right to exercise it. This higher level includes not only the right to discharge authority, but also the right to delegate it to someone else.

A corporate employee may have the authority, for instance, to approve invoices for payment within pre-set limits. An example would be having authority to approve invoices up to a thousand dollars for the company. Once the invoices are reviewed and approved by this employee, they are paid, with no higher authority required. The employee, however, probably does not have the right to delegate that authority to anyone else.

A general in the army may have been given a great deal of power but not the authority to pull a civilian off the street and make him a major in the army. Authority essentially always has limits, especially in the area of further delegation.

God is sovereign. He both creates and holds authority. Without limitation He delegates authority any time, in any manner, to any degree, and for any length that He so chooses.

When Christ delegated authority to the family, the government, and the church, He made it clear in no uncertain terms that all three institutions are critical for accomplishing His purpose. His delegation of authority not only equipped the three institutions so they could accomplish their assigned tasks, but just as important, validated their legitimacy and necessity.

Learning about the type and degree of authority delegated to these ordained institutions helps us to understand the proper role and function that God intended for each of them. Furthermore, those who have been given responsibility for these institutions are the ones who actually exercise the authority, doing so on behalf of their respective institution (and ultimately on behalf of God, whether they know it or not).

In summary, God created civil government and delegated to it the authority He intended for it to have to accomplish His purpose. Thus, with respect to the primary subject of this book, this means that those who hold the authority of civil government do so because God has purposed for it to be that way. It is God's absolute prerogative to delegate authority—in whatever manner, to whatever degree, and for whatever amount of time necessary to achieve His purpose. Returning to Romans 13:1, we are reminded that, "Every person [is to] be in subjection to the governing authorities. For there is no authority except from God, and those which exist are established by God" (Rom. 13:1 NASB).

You Can Hide, but You Can't Run

With the above verse in mind, let's look at two passages from Daniel. These Old Testament verses appear to have a universal, ongoing application consistent with Romans 13:1:

> . . . the Most High is sovereign over the kingdoms of men and gives them to anyone he wishes... (Dan. 4:17 NIV)

> And he changeth the times and the seasons: he removeth kings, and setteth up kings... (Dan. 2:21 KJV)

An interesting question immediately arises about some infamous and repugnant political leaders the world has endured, such as Hitler and Stalin. Did God choose them? Of course, we understand that events occurring by God's permissive will and actually being within God's perfect design are sometimes poles apart.

Both Germany and Russia had a significant Christian presence in their populace when these two wicked leaders ascended to power.

The Political Imperative

What was the record of Christian political influence during this time? Sadly, being Christian in name and Christian in truth are often two vastly different things. In regard to Hitler and Stalin, perhaps the question should not be, "Did God permit them to come into power" but, "Did *God's people* permit them to come into power?" Was there not a time, before it was too late, that Christians could have acted and changed history?

Going one step further, what if we consider the question, "Who was the worst, most corrupt political leader in history?" As Christians, we might nominate Pontius Pilate. Who else can match the equivalent act of sentencing and ordering the execution Jesus Christ—the innocent, perfect, sinless deity whose very character was love?

With that in mind, let's review the following passage from the Bible. Jesus is on trial before Pilate, who is interrogating Him. Initially, Jesus chooses to remain silent:

Pilate therefore said to Him, 'You do not speak to me? Do You not know that I have authority to release You, and I have authority to crucify You?' Jesus answered, 'You would have no authority over Me, unless it had been given you from above; for this reason he who delivered Me to you has the greater sin.'

(John 19:10-11 NASB)

Amazing! The authority that Pilate held to order the execution of Jesus, according to Jesus' own words, came from God. **Pilate woefully and wrongfully used his authority, which he will eternally regret, but Pilate's authority was legitimate, regardless how reprehensibly it was misapplied.**

In the last half of verse 11, Jesus says to Pilate, "For this reason he who delivered Me to you has the greater sin." Certainly we can all agree that what Pilate did was a sin. But what could possibly the "greater sin"? We will discuss this later, since it has a direct application to the subject of this book.

Also note that there is a difference between those who hold authority "for" civil government and those who hold authority "in" civil government. In my opinion, the best scriptural interpretation is that God delegates authority at the most fundamental level to those who

27

have the primary responsibility "for" civil government. Those who have authority for civil government have authority over those who are "in" government. In turn, all of them have a responsibility to God as individuals. **This is a key point that is fundamental to everything we say as we go forward in this book: in a system of government that, at its most basic level, is rooted in the right of the individual to vote and thereby collectively hold the right to self-govern; then the individual citizen is the primary holder of civil authority at the most fundamental level, and this is the authority that has been delegated directly from God.**

Let's think about what that means for a minute. For countries whose civil governments use a democratic system of elections to choose their political leaders, then citizens who are old enough to participate in the political process actually hold God's direct delegated authority for civil government. More specifically, it means that each citizen has actually been assigned by God a portion of His very own authority (Dan. 4:17).

What about presidents, senators, governors, and all those who have responsibilities in our civil government? Their terms and requirements to serve, along with the powers and responsibilities that go with their respective offices, exist only because we citizens say so, either through the U. S. Constitution, various state constitutions, or other legislation. Each state has two senators because we say so. A citizen of the United States must be at least thirty-five years of age to serve as president because we say so. Those who hold those offices for a certain period of time do so because we say so. The fact that we have offices called president, senator, governor, and mayor is all because we say so. And so it goes, throughout the breadth and depth of government—at every level.

But all of our governing documents establishing laws, including the U. S. Constitution, can be modified to any degree if enough individuals collectively want it. Moreover, the changes can be made in orderly, legal ways—without a revolution or rebellion. Is it difficult and time consuming? Yes, as well it should be. What should be clearly understood, however, is that the only unchangeable feature about our system of government at this point in the history of our country involves the ultimate authority of the individual.

The point here is not about making changes in our fundamental system of governance, but this: we cannot afford to view our system of government in any manner other than the biblical truth that *the individual citizen is the primary, fundamental holder of God's delegated, assigned authority.* This concept might not mean much to the non-Christian or nominal Christian, but to the biblical Christian, this is huge.

Christian Duty and Assignments from God

As Christians, when we receive an assignment from God, we must dutifully accept the task and then diligently pursue it until we are released from the assignment. A good working definition of Christian duty is this:

> God assigns—we accept.
> God expects—we respond.

Not much wiggle room is allowed there, nor should there be.

There are two parables that Jesus taught—one recorded in Luke and the other in Matthew—that have both similar and also distinctively different elements. The Luke parable is often known as the parable of the minas or pounds, and the Matthew parable is generally referred to as the parable of the talents.

We will focus on the similarities between the two parables for this discussion to gain insight about what it means for God's servants to have an assignment directly from their Lord. Below is the text from the two parables for our study:

> *Therefore He said: A certain nobleman went into a far country to receive for himself a kingdom and to return. So he called ten of his servants, delivered to them ten minas, and said to them, 'Do business till I come.'*
> *(Luke 19:12-13 NKJV)*

> *For the kingdom of heaven is as a man travelling into a far country, who called his own servants, and delivered unto them his goods. And unto one he gave five talents, to another two, and to another one; to every man according to his several ability; and straightway took his journey.*
> *(Matt. 25:14-15 KJV)*

The word rendered "servant" in these two parables comes from the Greek term doulos, but an equivalent, or perhaps better, translation would be the word "slave." Some Bible translations use the word "slave" rather than "servant." Think, then, about how a slave or servant responds to the command of the master. In both parables Jesus is referring to Himself as the Master. The message to His disciples concerns His impending departure, His non-optional assignments to His followers during His physical absence, and His certain return. It is the response of the servant (slave) to the command of his master that we need to completely understand.

In both parables we see the master calling his servants together, as was his right to do. We see the master making assignments, which was also his right to do. One question we might ponder is, what did the servants say? As far as we know about these two parables, the servants didn't say anything. This was not a focus group in which the topic was open for discussion.

Also note what did not take place. The master did not call his servants together and say, "Fellows, I have put together a list of things I want you to work on. Why don't you look over the list and see if there is anything that appeals to you. If you get a chance, you might work on the list some; otherwise, don't worry about it. When I get back, we'll see what we have yet to do and then work on it from there." Re-read the parables. That conversation never took place.

The master summoned, and the master assigned. Certainly we may presume that the master knew his servants well enough that he did not make any mistakes in his assignments. From the servants' point of view, however, it did not matter whether or not the assignments appealed to their desires. It didn't matter if it wasn't their "thing" or "within their comfort zone," or any other excuses that we sometimes use today as a filter to screen out the stuff we prefer not to do. Moreover, there were no complaints. Remember, God assigns—we accept; God expects—we respond. That is the nature of an assignment from God.

The next lesson we need to learn from these parables is that when God delegates and assigns, He requires a *personal, individual* account. The following verses talk about the return of Christ. We are taught in these passages that one of the things that Christ will do upon His return is to individually evaluate the performance of His servants. That evaluation will specifically focus on the assignments that He has called His servants to do.

> *After a long time the lord of those servants came and settled accounts with them.*
>
> (Matt. 25:19 NKJV)

> *And so it was that when he returned, having received the kingdom, he then commanded these servants, to whom he had given the money, to be called to him, that he might know how much every man had gained by trading.*
>
> (Luke 19:15 NKJV)

We shall also notice in the following verses that God takes His assignments to His servants very seriously. We need not find ourselves like the subject of the following verses, and hopefully we will not be. But consider the servant who was called, given a clear assignment along with ample opportunity to do it, and then, for whatever reason, simply did not perform it. These harsh judgments follow.

> *His master replied, 'You wicked, lazy servant! . . . . throw that worthless servant outside, into the darkness, where there will be weeping and gnashing of teeth."*
>
> (Matt. 25:26a, 30 NIV)

> *And that servant who knew his master's will, and did not prepare himself or do according to his will, shall be beaten with many stripes.*
>
> (Luke 12:47 NKJV)

Indeed, God takes His assignments seriously. Thus, with respect to Christians and civil government, it is appropriate now to fully integrate what we have learned so far:

1. God ordained civil government.

2. Christ created the institution of civil government (along with the family and the church) to be a vital, integral

ongoing part of His plan, in which He takes a continuing role.

3. The purpose of Christ's work on the earth was the initiation and establishment of a system to carry out the Great Commission. So, we now recognize and acknowledge that civil government holds some key role in the advancement of the Great Commission as surely as the family and the church, although not the same role. For the Christian, nothing is more important than fulfilling the Great Commission.

4. God is the ultimate holder and arbiter of all power and authority; moreover, He delegates authority and power as He pleases.

5. God has first created and then validated civil government via empowerment—the delegation of His very own authority to the institution of civil government—and therefore to those who have the fundamental responsibility for civil government.

6. In any country where the individual citizen is eligible to participate in the process of self-government, the individual is the first and fundamental holders of direct authority from God for civil government.

7. Because God is sovereign and He determines via delegation who holds civil authority at the most fundamental level, participation in civil government becomes an assignment from Him with respect to this institution.

8. God takes His assignments seriously, so His assignments also must be undertaken with the highest degree of seriousness by those who receive them.

9. Performance with respect to these assignments will be evaluated by Christ on an individual basis.

10. We are clearly instructed in Luke 12:47 that once we un-

derstand the "master's will" with respect to our assignments, we must "prepare and do."

11. With respect to civil government, public policy, and the political process, this simple set of instructions—"prepare and do"—becomes our political imperative.

12. As holders of authority for civil government at the most fundamental level, we understand that we have an assignment from God, a political imperative which compels us to properly follow through. Understanding the role and purpose of civil government and our political imperative leads us to seek the proper biblically-based response: to become a Great Commission Citizens.

TWO

The Great Commission Citizen

For we do not wrestle against flesh and blood, but against princi-
palities, against powers, against the rulers of the darkness of this
age, against spiritual hosts of wickedness in the heavenly places.

(Eph. 6:12 NKJV)

The Biblical Role of Civil Government

In order to understand the elements of being a Great Commission Citizen, we must first look at the role and then the purpose of
civil government from a biblical point of view. Because they are two
different concepts, each must be understood individually. We must
come to terms with the role of civil government before we can fully
appreciate the purpose, for it is the proper application of the role
that makes achieving the purpose possible.

Consider the following verses:

Therefore submit yourselves to every ordinance of man for the
Lord's sake, whether to the king as supreme, or to governors, as to
those who are sent by him for the punishment of evildoers and for
the praise of those who do good.

(1 Pet. 2:13-14 NKJV)

This Scripture reflects the two building blocks that provide the basis for civil government and define the proper role of this ordained institution. First of all, we are exhorted to recognize the legitimate authority of civil government. This is clear from the beginning of the verse with the instruction to "submit." Christians should further note that their willing submission to the government is for "the Lord's sake" because the institution of civil government belongs to the Lord. He created and then empowered it. He maintains and sustains His creation of civil government because it is essential for accomplishing His purpose.

The first building block in the proper role of civil government from God's design is contained in the clear, unequivocal phrase "for the punishment of evildoers." The second building block, evident in the phrase "praise of those who do good service," is translated "encourage those who do good service" in the Amplified Bible. This tells us that government has a role in providing a framework for good things to happen.

Note that the passage below also requires obedience to civil government and further identifies the same two points which set forth the distinctive role of civil government as God defined for His created institution.

> For rulers are not a terror to good works, but to evil. Do you want to be unafraid of the authority? Do what is good, and you will have praise from the same. For he is God's minister to you for good. But if you do evil, be afraid; for he does not bear the sword in vain; for he is God's minister, an avenger to execute wrath on him who practices evil.
>
> (Rom. 13:3-4 NKJV)

God's intended role for government, when properly operating in the manner for which He designed the institution, is this: a civil and social framework where that which is good is encouraged and can excel, while that which is evil is restrained and punished. This is the basic building-block structure in a properly designed and functioning civil government, and all that is proposed or undertaken should be referenced back to these two basic points.

Whether or not that which is proposed or undertaken is aligned with one of these two basics should be the first question asked and the first hurdle to be passed regarding the actions of civil government. Does the governmental action provide the framework for, encourage, and facilitate good things to happen, whether it is on a personal, social, or economic basis? Does the governmental action discourage, inhibit, restrain, and punish evil?

The Bible is not a detailed public policy handbook, but it does clearly spell out the two primary building blocks. Those responsible both for and in civil government are the policy-makers whose job is to implement these principles appropriate for the time, place, and circumstances over which this government has authority.

This being the case, then conversely, the worst government would be one that restrains and even punishes good, while making provision for evil to flourish. Woe to those who would create such an anti-Christ oriented government, completely corrupting God's institution, and using it for the exact opposite for which He intended. And since each one of us has an assignment from God with respect to our individual responsibility, then woe to us as well if our own government is exhibiting these evil tendencies and we are not doing all we can with our God-given opportunity to stop and reverse them.

If we are going to encourage and facilitate "good" and restrain and punish "evil," the question quickly becomes, "good" according to whom and "evil" according to whom? Who gets to decide? The answer, of course, is that since we are receiving our input and direction from biblical principles, then it is always going to be "good" and "evil" according to the standards we find in the Bible.

Since God established civil government, and God wants good to be promoted and evil to be restrained by civil government, then His standards should be used to evaluate the good along with the evil that will be subject to governmental action. Otherwise, we cannot be assured that government will achieve what God intended; in fact, we can be assured that it will not achieve His intended role and purpose and may actually attain the opposite result.

A note needs to be made here regarding the Christian's obligation to be obedient to the evil requirements of government. Most would agree that a point can be reached where individuals cannot obey certain laws of an evil government because the requirement would require a direct violation of their calling as Christians, based on biblical standards.

When you examine the context of the verses below from the fourth chapter of Acts, you will notice that they concern whether the disciples should follow man's law when it directly violates the mandate Jesus had previously given them. The issue regards the call of Christ to advance the Great Commission versus the command of the authorities to cease.

> *But Peter and John answered and said to them, 'Whether it is right in the sight of God to give heed to you rather than to God, you be the judge; for we cannot stop speaking what we have seen and heard.'*
> *(Acts 4:19-20 NASB)*

Similarly in the fifth chapter of Acts:

> *But Peter and the apostles answered and said, 'We must obey God rather than men.'*
> *(Acts 5:29 NASB)*

Biblical "submission" ideally is the proper response to the proper application of proper authority, all based on biblical principles. However, what is the biblically proper response to a less than biblically ideal authority? The answer is "submit," unless submitting requires you to directly violate God's command. Submitting to God always takes precedence over submitting to anything else, even when there is a conflict with one of God's ordained institutions. When the civil government is operating properly, there will never be a conflict between submitting to God and to government. Conversely, when the Christian determines that they must disobey civil laws, then he or she must be willing to pay the consequences and count it as suffering for Christ. The following verse from the Gospel of John reminds us:

> *Remember the word that I said to you, 'A slave is not greater than his master.' If they persecuted Me, they will also persecute you;. . .*
>
> *(John 15:20a NASB)*

As Christians, we need to understand these two key points: (1) we will not be exempt from the wrath of an evil government just because we are taking a righteous stance; and (2) sometimes we bring suffering on ourselves for reasons other than the ones named by Jesus. God recognizes and blesses those who stand for righteousness if it's for Jesus' sake, not when it's a result of our own foolishness or lack of judgment.

The areas of public policy, civil government, and the political process present their own challenges for Christians to always conduct themselves in a manner worthy of the name they represent. It is all too easy to fall into those negative techniques regularly employed in the political fray and do damage to the name and cause of Christ, and bring grief upon ourselves. We need to make sure we stay within the boundaries specified in the verse below.

> *Blessed are they which are persecuted for righteousness' sake: for theirs is the kingdom of heaven. Blessed are ye, when men shall revile you, and persecute you, and shall say all manner of evil against you falsely, for my sake.*
> *(Matt. 5:10-11 KJV)*

Our task here, however, is not to ask individuals to violate laws fostered by evil governments, even though Christians throughout history have faced that choice and so may we. In one sense, our purpose here is exactly the opposite: it is a call to participate in building a civil government that reflects the intended role of government based on God's design - a civil system in which Christians are blessed by being submissive to the government because the authorities are carrying out the proper role of this institution.

It is critical for us to understand that this ideal government begins with individual Christians submitting to God's assignment, which means accepting the primary responsibility of building and operating such a government. **God has blessed us with the opportunity and requirement to build the very government to which we must be submissive.** What an awesome blessing and incredible responsibility!

This is why we must completely understand the proper role of the government when we respond to our duty from God. After we have gained a clear understanding of the guiding principles for the proper role of civil government, we will surely be able to recognize when the opposing principles are at work.

These are the key elements that set forth the biblically based requirements of civil government:

1. A proper civil government, operating as God designed, is a public system of laws and regulations, undergirded by a judicial system, that is established and administered consistent with biblical principles.

2. A proper civil government will provide a positive environment for personal, family, community, social, and national good to flourish, while restraining and punishing that which is evil.

3. A proper civil government will appraise the standards of good and evil according to Judeo-Christian principles.

It will indeed be a blessing and delight to submit to that kind of government.

Harmony Versus Hostility

All laws inherently reflect some worldview or value system. Whether or not individuals will admit it or can articulate it, all laws intrinsically reflect some worldview, some value system, some system of right and wrong, or good and evil.

The contest that continually persists in society, and therefore in government, is this: whose ideas of right and wrong, or good and evil, will be the prevailing justification for accepting or rejecting laws, implementing rules and regulations, and making judicial rulings? The Bible has the only correct answer—God created and empowered civil government for His purpose. Thus, only godly principles and Judeo-Christian values found in the Bible can properly guide the successful operation of God's ordained institution of civil government.

By this we know that the biblical principles regarding right and wrong, or good and evil, give us the only reliable process to evaluate elected officials, candidates, political platforms, laws, and regulations—or any other of the elements relating to the aspects of government.

Yes, in civil government, as in many other areas of life, there may be an occasional issue that would allow one's personal preference to guide because there doesn't seem to be any clear biblical principle at stake. Those instances will probably be few and sometimes may appear so because we have not delved into the issue sufficiently. Clearly, however, when challenges to our Judeo-Christian value system are presented, then only decisions consistent with those Judeo-Christian principles can be acceptable to the Bible-honoring Christian.

Just as important (and this cannot be overemphasized), a proper civil government operating as God designed will be in harmony with and not hostile toward God's other two institutions—the family and the church. God would not design a civil government that conflicts with or opposes the other two institutions He created. All three were established to serve His purpose.

So, when the civil government undertakes action that is hostile to or undermines the church or the Christian family, we know that it is not properly functioning because it breaks the harmony in God's design. Such a civil government causes conflict and confusion among the domains of church, family and government, and according to 1 Corinthians 14:33, God is not the author of confusion. Such a government is broken and needs to be fixed. The system will not be fixed by those who think it is fine the way it is; nor will it be fixed by those who, even though they don't like it, refuse to respond to their God-given obligation to do something about it.

God, of course, does not set one of His institutions against the other because His order always produces harmony. The church, the family, and civil government each have distinctive roles. When the three fulfill their intended roles, there will be harmony among all three institutions—never conflict or confusion. The Father, the Son, and the Holy Spirit are always in perfect harmony. As Christians we are responsible for the church, the family, and civil government. We will never be able to attain that divine level of harmony, but the same principle applies, and our obligation is to totally dedicate ourselves to that mission.

Legislating Propriety

Even though all laws and their implementation are based on some worldview, some system of right and wrong, or some moral basis for classifying good versus evil, you'll still hear the argument from time to time that "you can't legislate morality." But you may also sometimes hear the more accurate counter-argument, "Well, you can't legislate anything but morality."

You certainly can't "legislate" the law of gravity, the laws of thermodynamics, or other fixed physical laws. So as it turns out, laws reflecting social standards of behavior rooted in some moral basis for right and wrong are about the only thing government can legislate . This is exactly what you would expect once you realize that civil government is an institution designed, created, and empowered by God to fulfill His intended role for it which is to produce biblically-based moral order within a civil structure.

In the strictest sense, it may be proper to say that we cannot legislate morality. The Bible says in Proverbs 23:7 (KJV) that "as a man thinketh in his heart, so is he…" We cannot know what anyone thinks deep down inside because that is known only to God and self.

Just as certain, however, civil government can (and does) legislate against behavior that violates some view of right and wrong. The prior Scripture from 1 Peter says that the role of government is to punish "evildoers," and similarly the earlier reference from Romans mentions that the civil government is "an avenger to execute wrath on him who practices evil." ("anti-social behavior.") So civil laws regulate impropriety or anti-social behavior. Notice in the reference from 1 Peter and Romans the emphasis on action (i. e., "doer" and "practice"). God judges the thoughts (Jer. 11:20), while God's ordained institution of civil government judges the action—ideally both by the same standard.

God's Purpose for Civil Government

One of civil government's most fundamental roles, from a biblical point of view, is to restrain and punish evil. To examine this concept in the context of good and evil, let us consider that evil, at its core, is contrary to good. Thus, the evil that must be restrained and even punished is that which violates biblical principles, opposes Judeo-Christian values, and is hostile to God's other two institutions—the church and family.

Following this biblical interpretation provides the ability to discern and evaluate policies, positions, political parties, platforms, candidates, legislators, legislation, and judicial decisions in a much more straightforward manner. Subsequently, our charge from God in this area is to create and operate His institution of civil government according to His standards becomes much more straightforward as well.

Over the last few decades, we Christians have been deeply troubled and distressed by the severe social ills plaguing our nation, such as abortion, attacks on the institution of marriage, and other anti-biblical issues. We can be grateful for the many Christians who have chosen to engage in the area of public policy and civil government in order to address these ills.

But the real desired result will happen not when a valiant few make an effort to affect legislation, but when the vast majority of Christians begin to understand that they, too, have an assignment from God to establish and maintain a civil government which reflects biblical principles, upholds Judeo-Christian values, and proceeds in harmony with the church and family.

For us as Christians, the only option is to undertake this task. We are not free to reject this assignment, because God has made it and provided the very opportunity to carry it out. God assigns, we accept. God expects, we respond. Each person's performance with respect to this assignment will be evaluated individually by Christ.

This is the key from a biblical point of view: When a nation has a proper civil government operating as God designed, then the family, the church, *and the Great Commission* can flourish and excel. *God's purpose for civil government is to provide the framework in which the Great Commission can flourish.*

This, of course, makes perfect sense once we understand that civil government was ordained by God: it was created, empowered, and placed under the authority of Christ for His purpose. Furthermore, the purpose for Jesus' earthly ministry was to initiate the Great Commission and establish it as the principal, primary ongoing work of those who would follow His way and do His will.

This is the reason why the issue of civil government is so critical and should never be considered secondary to, or outside of, the Christian life and walk. Nothing is more important to Christ than Great Commission success, and no one knows more how to accomplish that than Him. Because the family, civil government, and the church were created by Him and for Him, He intends for these institutions to function according to His design and be fully deployed on behalf of His purpose – the Great Commission.

It will be Great Commission success that changes lives on an individual level, and changed lives will change the culture and government, build stronger families and churches which will then bring about even more Great Commission success. A proper civil government fulfilling God's purpose will play a critical role in achieving Great Commission success. So, it is fundamentally necessary that Christians take the call seriously to advance the Great Commission by becoming active in civil government, in order to bring it into compliance with God's intended design.

For us as Christians, helping to form and shape civil government to reflect God's purpose is a non-negotiable responsibility but it should be one that we relish for Christ's sake in order to fulfill His Great Commission. We could likewise say that in order to optimize Great Commission success, the family and the church must also fulfill God's designed role for them; but virtually all of us know, understand, and accept that. Thankfully, much has been written and spoken within the Christian community on the subject of the church and the family.

Rest assured that nothing written in this book is intended to diminish the role of the church or the family in advancing the

Great Commission—quite the contrary. The purpose here is to raise awareness about the role of civil government so it can take its rightful place that God intended in the Christian life alongside the church and the family, thereby enhancing the opportunity for success on behalf of those who have long labored to advanced the Great Commission.

When God created the family, church, and government, He meant for all three institutions to fulfill their respective role in achieving His purpose. It is God's sovereign prerogative to assigned every one of us a role in each institution. Again, God assigns, we accept. God expects, we respond.

Precept and Example

Two passages in the Bible—one from 1Timothy and the other from the Book of Acts–will help to underscore this relationship between civil government and Great Commission success. We might call these two passages, precept and example. First, consider the passage from 1Timothy:

> *Therefore I exhort first of all that supplications, prayers, intercessions, and giving of thanks be made for all men, for kings and all who are in authority, that we may lead a quiet and peaceable life in all godliness and reverence. For this is good and acceptable in the sight of God our Savior, who desires all men to be saved and to come to the knowledge of the truth.*
>
> *(1Tim. 2:1-4 NKJV)*

At the outset, these verses offer great, straightforward advice: pray for people in general, and more specifically, pray for our leaders in civil government; furthermore, as some commentators suggest, pray for their salvation. Those are all outstanding instructions to take away from this passage. Praying for people's salvation, whether or nor they are government officials, is always a good thing. But to be true to this particular passage, we must understand that even though the ultimate outcome of this specific prayer here is for the lost to be saved, the immediate objective of this prayer is for the saved to be able to live up to the calling of

Christ in an unhindered manner. The gateway to Great Commission success lies in the individual Christian possessing both the desire and ability to advance that mission.

To clarify this concept in our study, let's analyze this passage with a slightly different approach—from the bottom up. First, verse 4 says that "God desires all men to be saved and to come to the knowledge of the truth." Being saved and coming to the knowledge of the truth sound like (and are) the two objectives of the Great Commission restated.

From Matthew 28:18-20, we recall the twin elements of the Great Commission: baptizing (as a result of people being saved) and teaching (the saved) the biblical truths which Jesus had taught. So, we can safely conclude from 1Timothy 2:4 that God desires Great Commission success. This certainly should not be a surprise to anyone since Christ was sent from heaven to earth for that very reason—to initiate and establish a system to fulfill the Great Commission. The Great Commission is not just God's "desire"; it is also His overriding desire with respect to our basic Christian mission.

Let's continue our upward trek through this passage. Verse 3 tells us that this is something "good and acceptable" in the sight of God, who desires Great Commission success. Since carrying out the Great Commission is the primary calling for us as Christian disciples, we need to understand what is "good and acceptable" toward this end, or "good and pleases God," as the Amplified Bible says.

That which is "good and pleases God" can be found in the last half of verse 2—"that we may lead a quiet and peaceable life in all godliness and reverence." In other words, it is pleasing to God when the Christian community can proceed with their lives according to the manner to which He has called them, because God has called all Christians to advance the Great Commission.

Moreover, from the perspective of this passage, it is clear who controls whether Christians can live their biblically-called life in an unhindered manner. It is society (the culture) in general (v. 1), and very specifically, those who are responsible for civil government ("kings and all who are in authority" [v. 2]). So, for the ex-press purpose of having a civil government and social structure that is in harmony with, or at least, not hostile to the Christian community, 1Timothy 2:1-2 calls the Christian community to prayer.

Regarding the subject of this book, 1Timothy 2:1-4 can be summed up with the following statements:

1. We are exhorted to implore God that the culture in general and civil government specifically will be in harmony with, or at least not hostile, toward the Christian life and walk.

2. When the Christian community is free to fully follow God's calling, including being free from the negative influence and impingement of an unbiblical government, then good things begin to happen from God's point of view.

3. The best thing that happens is Great Commission success.

4. This pleases God since advancing the Great Commission is God's ultimate calling and purpose for Christians in this life.

This passage serves to instruct and remind us in a unique way about how the civil government, as it relates to the Christian community, can greatly affect Great Commission success. The distinctive element that we are blessed with today is that God not only still calls us to the prayer and purpose of 1Timothy 2:1-4, but He has also provided us the opportunity (and the assignment) to be the answer to our own prayer.

Unlike the early Christian church who faced an oppressive social and political environment, we have an opportunity to create a civil government that fulfills the role for which the early church could only pray—and thereby advance the Great Commission.

The following passage from the ninth chapter of Acts provides another interesting insight for our subject.

> *Then the churches throughout all Judea, Galilee, and Samaria*
> *had peace and were edified. And walking in the fear of the Lord*
> *and in the comfort of the Holy Spirit, they were multiplied.*

> *(Acts 9:31 NKJV)*

The report was that the churches were "edified" (signifying internal growth) and "multiplied" (signifying external growth). External growth (people being saved, baptized, and added to the membership) and internal growth (Christians being taught, trained, and discipled in the ways of Christ) are, of course, the exact two elements of the Great Commission. So, these churches were experiencing Great Commission success.

The report from these early New Testament churches is the ideal one of any church. All church ministries and programs should support either one of these two fundamental goals: internal growth or external growth. And it wasn't just one church experiencing this type of explosive growth; it was "the churches." This move of God was broader than any one town, neighborhood, pastor, or other local church identifier. These are the key features that provided the environment for this ideal report: (1) they were walking in the fear of the Lord; (2) they were walking in the comfort of the Holy Spirit; and (3) they had peace, or as the NIV says, "enjoyed a time of peace."

To the best of their ability and in regard to elements that were in their control, these churches were fulfilling their role. We might say their spiritual "house" was "in order." Likewise, we will never have Great Commission success without strong Christ-honoring, Bible-believing churches. But there was an external element pointed out in this verse that is also a huge key: they were enjoying a time of peace.

Commentators tell us that historically these events recorded in Acts 9:31 occurred not too long after the conversion of Saul, an event that certainly would contribute to a more peaceful environment for the churches. Also, it may have been, as some commentators suggest, that Rome had a new emperor, so the general level of threatening activity against the Christians by the Jewish authorities had subsided, probably until the new emperor could assess the situation.

Whatever the reason, the New Testament record tells us that the environment changed with respect to Christians and the civil authorities from a time of aggressive persecution to a time of peace. This time of peace was extremely critical to the Great Commission success that this group of local churches was experiencing. All the elements were working together: the spiritual commitment of the Christians coupled together with the external element of peace because the authorities were not aggressively hindering the work of the churches.

Later in the life of the early New Testament church, Christians would once again experience severe persecution. But for now these churches enjoyed a time of peace with respect to the civil authorities, which was a key element to their success in carrying out the Great Commission.

Historically, when the church has experienced persecution, it has scattered and re-emerged in new places and new ways. But even though God can use for good that which was intended for evil, at the time of God's judgment no one will want the evil persecution of Christians credited to their account. Yet we will be blessed to have credited to our account those activities within the domain of civil government that we engaged in to help create a time of external peace and harmony to allow the church to flourish. Even though the early New Testament Christians had no real opportunity or hope to shape civil government, we certainly do today.

We need to have a deposit credited to our heavenly account regarding the effective way we have used our opportunity and assignment from God, with respect to the government, to create a civilized environment that is at peace with the churches (Acts 9:31): a civil government in harmony with and not hostile to God's other two institutions—the church and the family. This provides a fertile environment for Great Commission success.

Perhaps when Jesus said, "Blessed are the peacemakers," He was referring in part to those who help provide a peaceful civil environment for Christian families, Christian churches, and the Great Commission to flourish. We would be identified as one of the peacemakers to the degree that we diligently pursue our duty from God to help conform civil government to its God-ordained role and purpose. This is not our only job as Christians with respect to advancing the Great Commission, but it is a crucial one, as we have learned from reviewing the Scripture passages from 1Timothy and Acts.

Getting It Right

The family, the church, and civil government each have a distinctive role to play in providing the optimal environment for Great Commission success from a human perspective. But the unique roles of these institutions are not designed to be interchangeable with any of the others. So even though we understand from the Scriptures that civil government, in its proper God-ordained role, will enhance the advancement of the Great Commission and we have a responsibility to God to see that civil government conforms to that role, we should always understand these principles:

1. It is not the role of civil government to perform the mission of the church. As Christians, we don't want or need the government's help in performing the mission of the church.

2. It is the requirement of the individual Christian citizen, however, to advance the proper mission of civil government when God provides the opportunity.

3. It is the responsibility of the church to teach the difference.

Early American Precedent

The family, civil government, and the church were all established by God and placed under the lordship of Christ to achieve

Great Commission success. With that being understood, then the ideal situation for Great Commission success (which is our overriding call as Christians), would be a society and a country:

1. founded on Judeo-Christian values that are consistent with godly principles;

2. where the family, church, and civil government are in harmony with each other; and,

3. where each of these institutions properly reflect God's design and His delegated authority.

The best historical example of these elements is the United States of America. The USA is not and never was perfect by any standard, but as an example of the founding of a nation based on biblical criteria, America comes closest to the model, at least in its ideals. To a large degree, compared to most emerging countries, the United States has been insulated from any overpowering outside influence. So the U.S. serves as a laboratory to prove either the success or failure of the ideals on which it was founded.

The United States was initially founded by colonies, communities, and leaders seeking personal, family and religious freedom, along with political and economic freedom. Different groups and different people had different priorities. By and large, all of these groups were either basically or fervently committed to Christian principles. Regardless, there was an almost complete deference to the Judeo-Christian value system throughout the society, both in the culture and in government—and that is the key.

It should be pointed out here that economic freedom is an essential element of personal and political freedom. More than one of the founding colonies in America nearly failed because, despite their deep Christian faith, they attempted to operate within a closed communal economic system that was, essentially, economic socialism. This was, in effect, an attempt to merge the church and the family past their biblical boundaries. They survived only by abandoning their well-intentioned economic collectivism in favor of individual property rights, self reliance, and personal economic benefit based on a value-added system of risk, work and reward. Out of this foundation for economic progress then came the ability to create a sustainable economy, provide for the family, build some measure of personal prosperity, establish an inheritance, support the church and the government, and extend charity to those who needed help.

But, regardless of the glitches and inconsistencies, basically the country was founded on a system incorporating and reflecting elements of the biblical model we have been studying. And what happened? America soared as a nation, and within the nation the body of Christ also soared.

The churches became robust, vigorous, influential, and effective throughout the country. Charity abounded as Christian-based institutions that were established flourished. On a worldwide basis, the churches in the U. S. have been responsible for sending out and supporting more missionaries than any other country in history. Thus, the Great Commission was spread, both at home and abroad.

Critically, through the influence of the churches and the consciences of individual Christians, America demonstrated, in the case of slavery, that she could face her imperfections and self-correct. Slavery never fit our founders' model and was a blight on the nation from the outset. It truly was, and is, an anathema to a nation whose model for civil government is a biblically-based one. As a nation, there was an irreconcilable difference between our high principles reflected in the words of our founding documents and the abominable deeds we committed against our fellow human beings. Our high ideals and our low practices could not co-exist.

An inevitable collision course was set from the beginning. The U. S. either had to abandon our biblical model for civil government altogether, or abolish slavery altogether. There were people on both sides of that issue, even though they may never have viewed their disagreement in that way. As is always the case, the longer the delay in dealing with a problem, the more traumatic the correction. It was a tough self-correction, but it was, nonetheless, a *Christian-aligned* self-correction.

The Challenge Continues

The contest between those who would establish a biblically-based model for civil government versus those who would implement an anti-Christian model continues today, and will persist until the end of the age. To the degree that the Christian community is not continually engaging, reforming, and conforming civil government to fit the God-ordained biblical model, then those with non-Christian and anti-Christian views of society will begin to use civil government to set the rules. Eventually the depths of human depravity will begin to be legitimized and legalized, such as abortion and homosexual marriage.

Civil government is an extraordinarily powerful institution that will never be benign in itself. A certain set of predominating values will shape the culture by what is either permitted or restricted. When Christians are active in the areas of politics and government for the right reasons and using the right methods, then that will play a key role in advancing the cause of Christ, which is the Great Commission. Christians must become active in the political arena—not because it is government's role to advance the Great Commission, but due to the negative, depressing impact that an imperious government has on Christian families and churches. This is the lesson to be learned from 1Timothy 2:1-4 as well as from church history.

When we are not fulfilling our duty from God in the political arena, then sometimes our churches may seem to be more like spiritual hospitals that cocoon its members and spend substantial time and effort trying to patch up, and repair the damage done by an anti-Christian culture and government. Retreat and defeat, however, is not our calling from God.

Many suggest that America in now in a post-Christian era. Throughout most of the history of this country, overwhelmingly, people demonstrated a broad, general deference to biblical principles and the Judeo-Christian value system entrenched within the culture and civil government. Of course, not all of the citizens were Christians, and certainly not everyone acknowledged the

Bible as authoritative. Even so, history will show that the majority of Americans respected the biblical values established in our culture and laws.

But this is not the case today. In our modern-day culture, Bible-honoring Christians, biblical principles, and the Judeo-Christian value system are constantly ridiculed, rejected, cast aside, and overrun—not subtly or covertly in dark corners or in a sleazy sub-culture, but in a prideful, boastful, arrogant, and aggressive manner that is blatantly obvious. This vociferously anti-Christian movement is now mainstream in our society, across the board.

Sadly, if the question "Who lost America?" is asked from a Christian perspective, the answer has to be that we did. Then the accompanying question must be, what is our solution for re-asserting Christianity's role in America and undergirding, invigorating, and supporting the family, the church, and the Great Commission? What else needs to be joined to the tireless work this generation's Christians are faithfully undertaking? Perhaps along with all the other ministries in the church and family, we need to include one that focuses on civil government. We might try using all the tools God has given us and vigorously fulfill our assignment in this area as well.

Just as establishing a country that reflects the biblical model was hard enough for the founding fathers, living up to that model has also proved a challenge for each succeeding generation, certainly including ours today. But inherent within the country's founding model, because it was essentially a biblically-based one, was its built-in capacity to face serious issues and self-correct if the church insisted and individual Christians acted out their role as conscientious citizens.

That model will still work today. The key to self-correction for a nation using a biblically-based model involves the extension of Christian influence into the culture in general and civil government, specifically, which is one of our assignments from God. When the country is set on the right course from a biblical perspective, it enhances the opportunity for Great Commission success—our primary purpose as Christian disciples.

The Three-legged Stool

Even though God established the three great institutions of the family, civil government, and church to achieve His purpose, to a very great extent the Christian community today has mistakenly regarded only two of these institutions as vital to our Christian walk.

The family, the church, and civil government support God's plan like a three-legged stool holding up a great weight. But no matter how strong the two legs are, if the third leg is weak, only a limited amount can be supported.

As deeply concerned Christians, we have tirelessly labored away at our two-legged stool while we wonder why our culture continues to tilt. The problem is the third leg. We have, to a far too great degree, abandoned the third domain - the domain of public policy, civil government and the political process.

And where we have abandoned God's ordained institution, others have been all too willing to step in, to the detriment of the family, the church, and the Great Commission.

There is a harmony in God's creation, and He intends for all His creation to serve His purpose. When we think of God the Father, we think of God as creator, protector, and provider. Thus, we view the family, His ordained institution, as the surrogate to properly incorporate and reflect these attributes. When we consider God the Son, we think of His role as our savior and spiritual teacher, so we see this predominately reflected through His ordained institution of the church. The roles of God the Holy Spirit, among other things, are to guide, restrain, and convict. That surrogate role takes place through the government with respect to civil order by encouraging that which is good and restraining that which is evil.

All three institutions—the family, the church, and civil government—are fundamental for establishing the earthly framework to advance God's purpose. Chaos and confusion in the family, especially regarding what constitutes a family; lethargy and apostasy in the church; and civil governments hostile toward the family and the church are all enemies of God's plan. The source of this chaos and confusion is Satan, whose goal is to impede, to the maximum degree possible, the advance of the Great Commission.

Our Personal Imperative

But we have a political imperative, which is this: because God allows our participation in civil government, then He also requires our participation in civil government. It is the duty of God's people to bring His desire for civil government into conformity with His design for it. And as Christians, we must join in God's work with respect to civil government as He gives us opportunity. Colossians 1:17 (NASB) reminds us that with respect to His creation of civil government, ". . . in Him all things hold together." God always has been—and will continue to be—interested, active, and involved in His creation of civil government because it is crucial to achieving His purpose.

All Aboard

Moreover, there are two important things we should also remember regarding coming to terms with our political imperative: (1) the historical lack of opportunity for Christians throughout times past does not permit or excuse our lack of inaction in the presence of immense opportunity today; and (2) when it comes to being able to join God in advancing the Great Commission, we should always consider the opportunity He provides to be a blessing, not a burden.

> Then He said to His disciples, 'The harvest is plentiful, but the workers are few. Therefore beseech the Lord of the harvest to send out workers into His harvest.'
> (Matt. 9:37-38 NASB)

When God provides opportunity, He invites and compels us to join Him. There are various types of work and workers needed to advance the Great Commission. Our earlier review of the parable of Matthew 25 reminds us of that fact.

This passage from Matthew 9:37-38 is very interesting. We are exhorted to pray to the Lord to send (thrust out) workers. For instance, we need Christian parents committed to and motivated by His call. For the Christian family to survive amidst the amorality of the pagan world system, it must have fathers and mothers who will stand strong for godly values. Christian parents also must oppose the distractions, diversions, and destruction offered by the world, which can occur either with them, the children, or both. Praise God that there are millions of Christian parents who are dedicated to building Christian families!

We also need pastors, teachers, missionaries, and the full list of church workers who will continually strive to "keep the main thing, the main thing." They must evaluate all church programs, expenditures, and activities by this standard: Do they advance the Great Commission? Praise God that there are countless pastors, church leaders, and workers who are selflessly giving their lives, year after year, to this call!

Moreover, we need those who are willing to participate in the political process at a multitude of levels. Sadly, civil government is the God-ordained institution that is most neglected by Christians. This is due to the fact that we have not fully appreciated God's perspective regarding the ways this institution can advance His purpose.

This "thrusting out" referred to in Matthew 9:38 comes from being yielded to the Holy Spirit, who indwells every Christian believer. Being informed is simply not enough. Local churches and the Christian community at large need to pray for more workers to be thrust out. Then, they need to join that work by making sure that those called to each area of service (family, church, and civil government) are identified, encouraged, equipped, and sent out.

To effectively influence civil government, we will ultimately need to be thrust out of our homes and churches into a different environment—deep into the world of political process. Each local church has a role in the preparation and subsequent thrusting out of its Great Commission citizens into this process.

As Christians, we must be constantly reminded of the need to pray for and be properly submitted to our government officials. We all need this reminder, which applies to any time or place in history. It also applies whether or not we, as individuals, have any real responsibility for selecting or holding those officials accountable. In our form of government, however, it is the individual citizen who primarily holds civil and political authority. Therefore, it is the application of this authority that we must address today in the Christian community.

Our time and place in history provides us with a great opportunity in the area of civil government; therefore, our next step is clear. As we learned in Luke 12:47, we must "prepare and do." The following two verses join the Great Commission and the political imperative to create what we will call "the Great Commission citizen":

> *And Jesus came and spoke to them, saying, 'All authority has been given to Me in heaven and on earth.'*
>
> *(Matt. 28:18 NKJV)*

> *For the Son of Man is as a man taking a far journey, who left his house, and gave authority to his servants, and to every man his work, . . .*
>
> *(Mark 13:34a KJV)*

In giving the Great Commission (Matt. 28:18-20), Jesus started out by saying, "All authority has been given to Me in heaven and on earth." While teaching the disciples about His departure and return, Jesus said in Mark 13:34 that His authority would be given to His servants, and "to every man his work." Clearly, when Jesus delegates governmental authority to His servants, He intends for it to be dutifully accepted and diligently applied. That is part of His Great Commission provision: Christ will equip us with the opportunity and ability to accomplish His work.

Jesus has placed the authority for civil government in our hands, so it is time for us to become worthy stewards of that high calling. However, simply being in agreement with what is written here is not enough; it is what you do when you finish reading that counts.

THREE

The Missions Model

Though one may be overpowered, two can defend themselves. A cord of three strands is not quickly broken.

(Ecc. 4:12 NIV)

Your Way Works Best

Every local church can effectively establish a ministry whose main purpose is to help its members work together to become active in civil government, public policy, and our political process, as God leads. Such a ministry is an important undertaking, based on the scriptural understanding about a strong, non-negotiable Christian imperative for these areas.

Since few churches have such a program, I suggest that when a church initiates one, it should use what I call the "missions model." How does the missions model work? With mission work, ideally God calls people to this field, and the church then sends them out. But important things must happen between the calling and sending. That is, future missionaries must respond to the call, prepare themselves, and present themselves to the church as those who are ready to undertake the call, with God's grace.

Essentially all Christians and every church support missions. Some individuals are called to be full-time missionaries living away from their homeland. Many are called to state or national missions, others to local missions. Still, others go on short-term mission trips.

Sometimes, Christians are led to long-term neighborhood and

community missions. Some do mission work as a full-time vocation, with numerous dedicated workers serving on a volunteer basis. This is possible because the local churches and Christian community universally recognize God's ordained role for His people in this area. The church preaches and teaches missions—and then the church plans, initiates, endorses, prioritizes, nurtures, supports, prays for, emphasizes, recruits for, features, instructs about, and blesses missions.

When mission work is honored through a variety of formats and across all age groups year after year, the local church becomes rich, fertile ground for God's call to take root. Then, when God calls, there is both an individual and congregational response that results in mission work. This is the "missions model."

Churches can effectively adapt this missions model for civic activity within their own congregational structure. Pastors and local church leaders can preach and teach the principles of Christian civic responsibility such as the ones discussed in this book, and then identify, encourage, and make provision for those who have a specific call for this discipleship mission. Over time, the church can develop a core team from this group.

Leadership and organizational skills, spiritual maturity, boldness, time, commitment, patience, and certainly a passion for the purpose should all be traits that the individuals on the core team possess. This organization, operating under the authority of the local church, can develop expertise, nurture this mission, and assist other church members with finding and fulfilling their roles. This is a wonderful activity for singles or couples, men or women, and teens.

Finally, to fully implement an effective program, cooperating and coordinating with others outside your church membership will eventually become necessary. This is especially important as efforts move outside the church into the local community. In the political arena, coordination and cooperation are key elements to success.

Four Building Blocks to Success

Just as churches organize, operate, and conduct their ministries in various ways, the missions model can accommodate a variety of implementation methods. But to be effective, I believe that the program must be designed around these four building blocks:

1. A Christian's activity in public policy, civil government, and the political process is honorable, and needs to be recognized as such by church leadership. Any alternative results in suppressing Christians, as individuals, from fully engaging in this area and exercising a key part of their Christian life and walk.

We should not, within a local church, intentionally or unintentionally, directly or indirectly, separate the political process from our whole walk with Christ. A successful church ministry must first emphasize that participation in politics is honorable.

2. A Christian's activity in public policy, civil government, and the political process is mandated. We have learned this in the sections called "The Political Imperative and the Great Commission Citizen." Yes, the mandate depends on our individual opportunity, but it is also based on our God-given opportunity. If we fill our time and personal agenda with so many items that we don't have time for our assignment from God, then our self-restrained opportunity does not exempt us from the requirements of our God-provided opportunity.

When certain items compete for our preferences and priorities, then we know we must put what God wants ahead of the competition. It is critical for a successful church ministry to emphasize that participation in the political process is a biblically mandated priority.

3. The local church not only needs to establish a program, but it also needs to make sure the program is supported. The program must be validated on a continual basis by the entire church leadership. All church programs and

ministries require a certain amount of "care and feeding" by the senior church leadership to maintain them at an effective level. New programs need to be nurtured even more so. The leadership just can't start a program and then mark it off the checklist without supplying it with some maintenance and encouragement.

This ministry may be viewed as unusual and even controversial at first. That means the leadership should provide an even higher level of initial support. Even before the initial committee is formed, a good measure of preparation for success needs to be made by teaching the church members the principles of the political imperative and the Great Commission Citizen. The moment the church senses that the leaders don't really enthusiastically support this ministry, it will begin to dwindle and then die.

One good thing about a Christian citizenship ministry is that it doesn't cost much budget money to operate. There are actually very few things that the church can spend money on in the areas of the political process. Nevertheless, an investment of high-level, non-monetary support is vital. So a successful program will be one that is truly supported at the working level, and known to be supported throughout the church leadership, especially by the pastor.

4. Drawing again on the missions model, the effective program will be a gateway. The church is certainly the proper venue for teaching and training Christians with respect to public policy, civil government, and the political process. However, most of the implementation will occur outside the church, in the community.

Much of the grassroots political activity is done within political parties and on a partisan basis. That is the way our country is organized. But partisan political activity must be exercised outside the formal church organization. Workers in this area must be "sent out" and initially perhaps "thrust out" (Matt. 9:38). The sending is essential. Theological and philosophical agreement, along with intellectual assent about the way things should be done, is not enough. The good news is that those whom God has truly called to this ministry will be anxious to participate, with just a little training and a little encouragement. A successful ministry will, as much as anything else, be a gateway for individuals to take the tools developed through training at church and enter the domain of the political process.

Political Parties

Our political system has two dominant parties, Democratic and Republican, with third parties coming and going from time to time. Individuals engaging in the political process will ultimately need to choose to actively participate in one of these parties. If one party becomes unsuitable for some reason, then a person can try a different party. One's Christian principles must serve as the guide, and that must override any other associations, affiliations, or traditions.

> *Beware lest any man spoil you through philosophy and vain deceit, after the tradition of men, after the rudiments of the world, and not after Christ.*
>
> *(Col. 2:8 KJV)*

No political party "owns God." Indeed, all political parties can benefit from the presence of strong Christians bringing Judeo-Christian principles into the system in a positive but uncompromising way.

Sometimes it is suggested that people compromise their principles, and certainly we hear of this in the political realm. However, I am more of the opinion that people rarely, if ever, actually compromise their most fundamental principles; but under pressure and conflict, they merely reveal what their true principles are. Only that which we will not compromise under pressure and conflict can be considered a foundational principle. That is why we must be certain that the political decisions we make are fully consistent with biblical principles and the Judeo-Christian value system. Even though times, circumstances, issues, political parties, and people change, our Bible does not.

How do we apply biblical principles to civil government? Here is an example: Abortion is morally wrong and violates biblical standards because it is the wrongful taking of a human life made in the image in God (Gen. 9:6). Thus, regardless of the person, the political party, or our relationship to either one; any candidate or elected official who tolerates abortion as a desirable, civilized, or acceptable social or public policy is unfit to be elected or appointed to any public office in any capacity, and thus should never receive any vote or support from us as Christian believers — regardless of party affiliation. The Great Commission Citizen will always, unequivocally and unapologetically, follow that principle.

No Invitation Necessary

We pray for the day when all political parties will actively appeal to Christians through their candidates and party platforms. Our job, however, is not to wait for change; it is to create change. Thankfully, we don't have to wait until we are invited because the door is already open.

Every elected public official and political party officer— national, state, and local—will be up for election at least once within the next six years, and some multiple times. Because the system is wide open, we are free to choose which political party we participate in, and we can switch parties each election if we want to.

The Push to a Call

What does God want us to do? Not everyone is called to do the same thing in the political process, just as we are not all called to the same role in other areas of our Christian lives. But each individual has a definite role.

Personally, I have been actively involved for over thirty years in most of the elements of grassroots political involvement. Does that mean that I believe every Christian should do what I do? If so, then those who faithfully, year after year, sing in the choir or teach third-graders in Sunday school have the right to expect me to get involved in their ministries to the same degree that they do. Both the choir members and the third- graders will be glad to know that

I am going to do neither because I am not called to those ministries.

The local church honors and supports singing in the choir and teaching children, as well they should. Those who may sense God's call to serve in these areas are supported and blessed by the church in their decision. Their call is validated by the local church body, which recognizes the importance of these roles to achieve its objectives.

God calls people into service in a variety of areas within each of His ordained institutions. Moreover, just as He gave some servants multiple tasks, as we read about in the earlier parables, some Christians today may be called into service in more than one of His institutions. It is important for the churches and Christian community to help each person to identify their call from God and support them so they can succeed in that call.

Thus, we need a specific ministry within each local church that is dedicated to helping its members understand the proper role of the individual Christian in the political sphere, as well as how it relates to the greater purpose of Christ and the Great Commission. Then, that local church ministry needs to serve as a gateway for placing individuals into their called area of service outside of the church, into the civil domain.

Like many organizations, churches have elements within their operations that reflect or approximate the well-known 80/20 rule. For instance, 20 percent of the membership may provide 80 percent of the financial contributions, and the remaining 20 percent of the contributions may come from the remaining 80 percent of the membership. In the same respect, 80 percent of the lay activity in the church is probably done by 20 percent of the membership, and the remaining 20 percent of the work by the remaining 80 percent of the membership.

Perhaps your church is an 85/15 church or a 75/25 church. The exactness of the 80/20 numbers is not as important as the concept. If a disproportionate few of the membership are providing a disproportionately large part of the ministry, then a large number of people are highly underutilized (along with some people being overworked). Yes, that probably occurs for a variety of individual reasons, such as spiritual immaturity or cluttering our lives with activities that excessively occupy our time. However, please consider that one reason some members are underutilized could be that their local churches are not offering the ministry to which they are called by God to undertake.

When a church begins to offer a dedicated ministry to implement programs that from a biblical perspective (1) teaches the elements of Christian citizenship; and (2) trains, encourages, and facilitates effective individual church member involvement in the political process, then a number of people who up until now have been far too inactive will be called into active service.

Appendix "A" gives a description of a Christian Citizenship Committee. Each church needs to establish such a committee (or the equivalent, depending on the customs and procedures of each local church) to implement the goals discussed in the previous paragraph. Then the Christian Citizenship Committee, with full support of the church leadership, needs to establish a Great Commission Citizens Corps within the congregation to be trained and led into these critical under-addressed areas of our Christian life and walk.

It is critical for the church to understand that it is not just the committee members alone who need to engage in the political process, but also the membership at large. And many members will, if within the church, such a calling is preached and taught as honorable and biblically mandated. The local church also must serve as a gateway through a dedicated ministry to train up and thrust out those who, with God's grace, will receive that message.

Remember, always honor biblical principles. Being involved in the political arena is not about power. It is not about partisanship, your pocketbook, or any political party; instead, it is all about your Christian principles and pursuing Christ's common call to Great Commission success.

FOUR

Objections and Reservations

Unless the LORD builds the house, They labor in vain who build it;
Unless the LORD guards the city, The watchman stays awake in
vain.

(Ps. 127:1 NKJV)

This would be an appropriate time to discuss some of the traditional objections and reservations to the idea of Christians becoming highly involved in the breadth and depth of the politics. It is the contention of this book that we are compelled to do so for Christ's sake.

Moreover, the suggestion here is that the local church should take the lead in teaching and training people how to become effective in civil government, which is part of God's design for Great Commission success. Because we are expected to respond based on a God-given call to a God-given opportunity, then the training required to be successful in this area is an appropriate and required function of the local church.

Other than having never really been taught these concepts, the reasons that Christians do not engage themselves in the political process generally include the following:

1. Historically, the church has not emphasized political/

civic involvement.

First, we must understand that Jesus was and is the most political person in all history, but not in the negative, cynical sense with which we often associate the term "political." He was political in that He created civil government for Himself, then set forth the purpose of the institution, and actively sustains its workings today.

Politics is the essence of the process by which civil governments form and function. Thus, Jesus created politics, and politics is part of His personal activity that continues within our time and place in history. He has called us and given us the opportunity to carry out His work in a manner that advances His role and purpose for civil government. That is politics. Our political participation relates to the high order of politics modeled by Jesus. We must not be reluctant or resistant to answer His call; instead, with a yielded spirit, we must seek out what that entails.

In the Old Testament, God's people operated through God's government via God's leaders to assist in accomplishing God's purpose. Certainly in the Old Testament we cannot help but see the intertwining of God's purpose for His people through His implementation of the governmental structure (which one would expect in a theocracy).

But also, in the New Testament Book of Acts, we definitely see Paul using the elements of government available to him to advance his missionary work. In Acts 16:37 Paul obtains relief against false imprisonment and illegal punishment by informing the authorities that he is a Roman citizen. In Acts 25:11, Paul uses his citizenship rights again to secure an appeal and assert his right to a fair trial.

Those Christians who belonged to the early New Testament church never had an opportunity, and thus never the obligations that we have today regarding civil government. Even so, based on these limited examples, a clear biblical precedent is evident: God's people can operate within their legitimate citizen rights appropriate to their opportunity, as well as their time and place in history, to advance their God-given ministry.

Throughout most of the history of the church, Christian citizens have rarely enjoyed the benefits of an open political system.

So, they were never able to embrace the circumstances and exercise the authority that we can as Americans citizens. This historical lack of opportunity for many should never be used to excuse the duty of those who are now blessed with opportunity. In fact, quite the opposite is true.

> *. . . For everyone to whom much is given, from him much will be required; . . .*
>
> *(Luke 12:48b NKJV)*

Frequently within the history of the Christianity, and continuing to this day in some areas, we see conflict and persecution of Christians and local churches directly by hostile governments or, permissively, by their citizens —certainly with negative results for the church. But as the early church grew throughout history, one of the accompanying events which occurred was that civil governments began to accommodate, then incorporate, and reflect Christian values within their own systems. That was always beneficial to the spread of the gospel. Then, at times civil government and the church became too close and too interrelated — far too often with negative results. (We will have an opportunity to discuss more about the "separation of church and state" later in this book.)

But history teaches us one thing: The Christian church and civil government cannot both thrive when they are in conflict. One will rise at the expense of the other, unless according to God's plan, they are operating in harmony with each other. In other words, each institution is properly functioning within their own God-ordained domain.

By design and as experienced throughout history, the institution of civil government has shown itself to be structurally the most powerful of God's three ordained institutions. When conflicts arise between church and state, it is not uncommon for governments to use its force to suppress the church. This is true both historically and today.

Clearly, churches that honor Judeo-Christian values and governments hostile toward these values cannot co-exist in harmony. In such a conflict, because government is more powerful, Christians suffer.

It should also be stated here that some persecution of Christian churches has been at the hand of other Christian groups who have misused the power of government to suppress and oppress others over doctrinal differences. Just because "Christians" control the government does not mean that everything it does reflects Christian values. This happens when there is, in effect, an attempt to merge the church and civil government past their biblical boundaries. That is why understanding God's role, purpose and boundaries for civil government is critical. It is also the reason that Christian character counts.

There is nothing Christian about some believers using the force of government to suppress other religions, different Christian denominations, or the secular non-religious. But there is also nothing Christian about rejecting God's call to join Him in His work when that involves the application of the God-ordained role and purpose for civil government according to biblical principles.

2. We can't save the world through legislation. The job of the church is the Great Commission, which means preaching and teaching the Bible, ministering to people's basic needs, and proclaiming the gospel for Christ. Ultimately, only that will make the difference.

Amen! However, one of the greatest impediments to the church, the family, and the Great Commission worldwide involve hostile governments, and vice versa (1 Timothy 2:1-4; Acts 9:31). We don't need to just look at history for examples, but at current events as well. There is still much persecution of and hostility toward the church on the part of governments today, with the same predictable results. For instance, one just needs to compare the health of the church in North Korea with the one in South Korea. Civil government matters.

Even though we are not responsible for other governments, we are responsible for our own. If our government is hostile to or not in harmony with the family and the work of the church, and we can make a difference, then we have a specific obligation to do so and thereby advance the Great Commission. It is not about any political party, but a conflict of worldviews that ultimately cannot co-exist.

3. Jesus said that His kingdom is not of this world (John 18:36).

Participating in public policy, civil government, and the political process is not about ushering in Christ's physical kingdom. There will be a time when Jesus establishes His rule on earth. We will be with Him, but He won't need our help (Rev. 19). One day, the Bible teaches, Jesus will have an earthly physical kingdom, but today He has a spiritual kingdom that He is expanding through the Great Commission.

Christian political activity has nothing to do with ushering in Jesus' physical reign and rule on earth, a role which He has reserved for Himself. Yet Christian political activity has everything to do with carrying out the Great Commission, a role which He has given to us. Understanding the political imperative and becoming a Great Commission Citizen involve the acceptance of a God-given assignment relating to a God-created institution that was established for a God-given purpose.

Who wants Great Commission success more than God? Who knows how to achieve Great Commission success more than God? We know the answers to those questions, so we should not doubt God. Instead, we should honor Him by using the full spectrum of God-created, supplied, and mandated tools—along with our opportunity, time, and place in history—for His calling and purpose. For us today that includes civil government to the degree that He gives us opportunity. It is our job to understand why and how; then we must prepare and do.

4. . . . .Then saith he unto them, Render therefore unto Caesar the things which are Caesar's; and unto God the things that are God's.

(Matt. 22:21b KJV)

70

It is wrong for Christians to suggest that civic engagement is commendable, but still declare, "After all, it is merely rendering unto Caesar, and not on par with church and family activity that we render unto God." Nothing could be further from the truth.

Yes, we do "render unto Caesar" certain things. We pay taxes and obey laws. We follow ordinances and comply with regulations, even when we don't agree with them. But we can be certain about this: when we get involved in civil government as Christians for the right reasons, we are not "rendering unto Caesar"; instead, we are "rendering unto God" in the fullest sense.

In the United States, the law requires a young man, upon reaching eighteen years of age, to register with the Selective Service System. However, the law does not require anyone to register to vote, or actually vote; to work in a political campaign; to become informed on the issues; to run for office; or do anything else politically. Frankly, "Caesar" would be happy if you never did any of these.

When you become engaged in the political process, however, you are "rendering unto God." It was God who created civil government for His purpose, legitimized its authority, and placed the responsibility and accountability in your hands.

As Jesus was teaching the lesson in Matthew 22:19-21, He told the Pharisees to bring Him a denarius. At Jesus' direction, they examined the coin and confirmed that it was bearing Caesar's likeness and inscription. Then, Jesus instructed them to render to Caesar the things that are Caesar's and to God the things that are God's. That lesson still stands and applies to our topic.

The denarius was created at Caesar's command, for Caesar's purpose, and bears Caesar's stamp. On the other hand, civil government was created at God's command, for God's purpose, and bears God's "stamp" as His ordained institution to establish order, restrain and punish evil, and provide the framework for good to prosper and excel. God's "stamp" is the empowering of civil government by delegating His very own authority to this institution so that it can accomplish its intended role. We render unto Caesar when we submit to civil government. **We render unto God when we submit to God by bringing His ordained institution of civil government**

71

into compliance with His ordained role and purpose for it.

5.   I vote. Get off my case.

In marriage, wedding anniversaries are important, and we understand that very well. I am sure that anyone who has ever forgotten an anniversary will testify to that. But suppose a husband celebrated a great anniversary with his wife by giving her flowers and gifts along with taking her out to dinner (the works), and then he absolutely ignored her the rest of the year. That would hardly qualify as the biblical basis for building a successful marriage.

Worship services on Easter Sunday always have the largest attendance of the year for virtually every church. Pastors are always grateful for every person that comes to the Easter services. But great churches are not built by those who only attend church on Easter Sunday and are not seen or heard from until the following Easter.

Clearly, attending church once a year at Easter cannot possibly be considered the Christian's full duty to the church. Certainly, showing up at home once a year for an anniversary cannot possibly be viewed as the Christian's full duty to marriage. And as positive as it is, the single act of voting once every year or two in no way qualifies as full performance of our duty in the area of civil government.

With the family and the church, one must fully understand their biblical purpose. Then, the individual must be completely dedicated to making these God-ordained institutions fulfill their respective roles. In other words, as Christians, we have to work at having a good marriage and a good church. The same holds true for God's ordained institution of civil government.

The political process has its own calendar, its own rhythm, to some degree its own lingo, and, in fact, its own sub-culture. We will never effectively manage to bring civil government into conformance with God's intended role by only engaging ourselves in the very tail end of the process known as voting. Even though voting is an honorable, vital, and commendable necessity, the complete task requires much more. This is why each church needs a Christian

Citizenship Committee: to understand the system, with its calendar and expectations, as well as entry and execution points that would allow effective participation for a variety of people with many different callings. This then, becomes each church's Great Commission Citizen Corps.

6. Separation of church and state is a biblical principle.

To have a coherent dialogue about this issue, one must first define the terms to be discussed. The Bible teaches that there is a distinction between the church and state. Each institution has a domain, although not a mutually exclusive one. The church should not attempt to be the state, and the state should not try to fulfill the role of the church or use the force of government to establish an official government religion or special church group within a favored religion. Government also should not serve the role of a secular "pseudo-religion."

Even though non-Christian individuals and families can be separate from the church, neither the family nor the church can be completely separate from the sphere of civil government because both of them exist within the boundaries of the state. The position and power of the state are such that it can be, and often is, pervasive in our lives. The government usually insists on having its own way and certainly has the power to enforce its wishes.

One of the reasons that Christians misinterpret the separation of church and state issue is due to the conflict and persecution that has historically occurred when one religion (or even one Christian faction) uses the power of the state to try to dominate or eliminate another Christian faction, sect, group, or denomination. We rightly resist and reject that abuse of power. But at the same time, we must not commit the classic mistake of "throwing the baby out with the bath water."

If the separation of church and state means that Christians must abandon their requirement from God to conform civil government to its biblically intended role, then we must reject that notion because that would be contradicting the Bible. By the way, such a fallaciously construed position isn't found in the U. S. Constitution, either.

Suppose Person A thinks there should be laws against stealing, basing that decision on biblical principles (Ex 20:15, Lev 19:13, Pr 11:1, Luke 3:13, Eph 4:28) . It doesn't matter, from a separation of church and state analysis, whether Person B (a secular atheist) agrees or disagrees with Person A. Person B has no real basis for claiming that Person A is attempting to impose a religions view simply because of the process by which Person A reached the decision. The issue of stealing crosses cultural, religious and philosophical boundaries. What if Person A and Person B completely agree? Was the conclusion by Person B valid because only non-religious values and principles were used, but the same decision by Person A is invalid because Christian values were used to influence the conclusion?

When civil government, operating within its proper role, is administered based on Judeo-Christian values, that does not constitute the imposition of a statement of faith or religious participation of any kind on anybody. It is not the role of civil government to favor or advance a particular religious doctrine or force participation in it on the citizens. However, properly standing guard against those who would use the power of civil government to advance a state-based religion does not mean that we should avoid our mandatory responsibility to make civil government conform to the role assigned to it by Christ. It is the role of the local church to understand and teach the difference.

God did not intend for the government to be a substitute for or duplicate the roles of the church or the family, or vice versa. That is not God's design. Each institution is distinctively created to complete God's whole plan. However, we will never fully experience that which God intended for the family and the church until we step up to the full measure of responsibility He has assigned us in the area of civil government.

7.   Politics is sleazy, worldly, and basically not for Christians.

One of the great issues that the early Jewish Christians, including the apostles, had to come to terms with concerned the treatment of Gentile Christians. Was there such a thing as the extension of Christianity to the non-Jewish people? If so, did the Gentiles have to enter into Christianity through the gateway of Judaism? Within the Christian community, what was the relationship between "God's chosen people" and the others once they became Christians?

Such was the dilemma Peter faced in Acts 10. In Peter's traditional, religious, and cultural framework, there was a clearly understood, unbreachable distinction that existed in regard to food considered (ceremonially) clean versus food thought to be unclean. A parallel distinction existed with respect to members of the Jewish race and those who were not—the clean and the unclean.

When God intended to clearly communicate to the early New Testament church His plan to extend Christianity to the Gentiles, He visited the apostle Peter in quite a dramatic way.

By the direction of God, Cornelius, a Gentile from a nearby town, had sent an entourage to invite Peter to his home. God's purpose was for Peter to share the gospel of Jesus Christ with Cornelius, his family, and friends. But first, Peter had to come to terms with the issue of clean versus unclean regarding his fellow members of the human race who were not Jewish. God forced Peter to confront a religious tradition that he felt he understood with absolute certainty, but was just not true.

As the delegation sent by Cornelius approached the house where Peter was staying, we pick up the action:

About noon the following day as they were on their journey and approaching the city, Peter went up on the roof to pray. He became hungry and wanted something to eat, and while the meal was being prepared, he fell into a trance. He saw heaven opened and something like a large sheet being let down to earth by its four corners. It contained all kinds of four-footed animals, as well as reptiles of the earth and birds of the air. Then a voice told him, 'Get up, Peter. Kill and eat.' 'Surely not, Lord!' Peter replied. 'I have never eaten anything impure or unclean.' The voice spoke to him a second time, 'Do not call anything impure that God has made clean.' This happened three times, and immediately the sheet was taken back to heaven.

(Acts 10:9-16 NIV)

The Political Imperative

Following this message from God and upon an invitation from the delegation, Peter agreed to go to the home of Cornelius. The following verses show that when Peter reached the home of Cornelius, he made it clear that he had not only received a message from God, but he had also understood the message.

> Talking with him, Peter went inside and found a large gathering of people. He said to them: 'You are well aware that it is against our law for a Jew to associate with a Gentile or visit him. But God has shown me that I should not call any man impure or unclean. So when I was sent for, I came without raising any objection.'
>
> (Acts 10:27-29a NIV)

The result was an evangelistic success accompanied and validated by the Holy Spirit, just like at Pentecost.

However, Peter's initial experience—after following God's call in this breakthrough ministry to the Gentiles—was to be criticized by his fellow church members at Jerusalem (the Jewish Christians):

> The apostles and the brothers throughout Judea heard that the Gentiles also had received the word of God. So when Peter went up to Jerusalem, the circumcised believers criticized him and said, 'You went into the house of uncircumcised men and ate with them.'
>
> (Acts 11:1-3 NIV)

Following that "welcome," the undeterred Peter gives them a detailed account of his vision, along with his experience at the home of Cornelius. At the conclusion of Peter's testimony, he offered this final piece of validating evidence:

> As I began to speak, the Holy Spirit came on them as he had come on us at the beginning. Then I remembered what the Lord had said: 'John baptized with water, but you will be baptized with the Holy Spirit.' So if God gave them the same gift as he gave us, who believed in the Lord Jesus Christ, who was I to think that I could oppose God?
>
> (Acts 11:15-17 NIV)

After this crucial meeting, the Bible says that those who heard Peter's testimony ceased their complaints and objections; instead, they praised and glorified God for this new truth they had now come to understand (Acts 11:18).

Even though the Old Testament prophesied the extension of God's calling to the Gentiles (Gen. 12:2-3, Isa. 11:10), Jesus pointed to it (John 10:16), and the early church leaders eventually agreed to it, the Christian Jews still had a hard time with it. It is one thing to finally see a truth in the Scriptures and even assent to the truth intellectually, even though it runs counter to that which we have been taught and led to believe. But sometimes it is an altogether different matter to act on the truth because it requires an internalization that is substantially deeper than intellectual assent.

The parallels to our subject with regard to Christian involvement in public policy, civil government, and the political process are obvious. The first thing we need to remember about civil government is that it is God's creation, not man's. God did not create government dirty, untouchable, tainted, unworthy, or unclean, but rather as clean, open, proper, and fitting for our full immersion into the breadth and depth of all its elements.

Are there untrustworthy people doing sordid things in government? Certainly, and the fewer Bible-honoring Christians involved, the more abusiveness there will be. Sadly, sometimes parents and even preachers fail and fall short. Nevertheless, the Creator of the church and family established these institutions to be godly. He intends the same for His creation of civil government as well.

In addition, as soon as one challenges the established paradigm, regardless of the scriptural soundness of the position, criticism will inevitably come next (Acts 11:2). Within certain bounds, there is nothing wrong with that. God bless those who take doctrine seriously enough to challenge any issue that has not yet, in their minds, passed the test of scrutiny in the light of the Scriptures. And bless those in the early church, who by the grace of God were able to advance past their deeply held beliefs on the subject of clean versus unclean and support the new paradigm.

You will be challenged, but simply be prepared to present the biblical basis for the political imperative and the Great Commission Citizen. Pray that God will allow you to present these truths to those who love His Word as much as you do. It is the work of the Holy Spirit to make them receptive and open their understanding to the message.

A final thought concerns something we might call "the compelling case of identical divine confirmation." When Peter recounted his experience regarding Cornelius, he concluded by pointing out that, based on their belief in Jesus, the Holy Spirit came upon the Gentiles in the same manner as He did on the Jewish Christians at Pentecost. Peter's conclusion was that if God provided the Gentiles with the same validation for the vital gift that He had already given the Christians in Jerusalem, then "who was [he] to think that [he] could oppose God?" (Acts 11:17 NIV).

The institutions of the church and the family were designed, created, and empowered by God. God holds all the authority but delegated a designated measure to the church and the family. The authority appropriate for each structure to accomplish its role has been assigned to each institution. Thus, we find this principle demonstrated: when God delegates His authority to an institution, He thereby validates it, and vice versa.

Likewise, this same validating process exists for the institution of civil government because it was also designed, created, and empowered by God. We clearly and indisputably recognize God's validating hand in the creation of the church and the family. Now we can just as clearly see the same validating hand in the institution of civil government. Just as with the church and family, God validates government through empowerment.

Once again, remember that God created civil government through Christ for His purpose, and then gave Christ lordship over it. Also remember not to call anything impure that God has made clean. Never hold in disdain or call something unfit, unclean, or unsuitable that which God has made clean, purposeful and a priority.

FIVE

God Bless America

For I know the plans I have for you, declares the LORD, plans to prosper you and not to harm you, plans to give you hope and a future.

(Jer. 29:11 NIV)

Provision and Appropriation

We often hear expressed, especially in Christian circles, about how God has blessed America. It appears to be an oft-repeated refrain, frequently stated with the accompanying concern that if America (the nation as a whole, or perhaps, at least, the Christians) fails to act in a certain way, we stand in danger of losing the "blessing." I would like to join in this discussion, but from a somewhat different perspective.

Has God singled out the U. S. for a special blessing? If so, what is that blessing? Can we lose it? Have we already lost it? How can we know?

Generally, God's blessing can be regarded as a special benefit or favor bestowed upon those to whom He chooses to grant this kindness. But with respect to God's blessing and America, how are we to best understand this blessing?

"The Wonderful World of Disney" television program has undergone many changes, including its name, over the years. In the early days of color television, it was officially called "The Wonderful World of Color." I remember the opening featuring a dark and somewhat vague outline of the Disney castle. Then Tinker Bell would dart in, flick some pixie dust on the scene to make everything burst into color, and the show would begin.

I'll have to admit there have been times my thoughts about God's blessing seemed to proceed in a similar manner. Under this view, America is blessed because God spread His "blessing" over America, which caused wonderful things to begin to happen. Perhaps America received this blessing because of the strong Christian commitment permeating the fabric of the nation. However, as this national commitment to Christian values wanes, then it may no longer please God to extend His blessing. As a result, the blessing may be partially, or even completely, removed. That view is not totally without biblical justification; Jeremiah 18:6-10 would be an example.

But today God is more than just among His people (as in Jeremiah's time); In this church age, as Christians, God is within us. So I would like to suggest another viewpoint. This viewpoint is that God's blessing follows what we might call a "provision and appropriation model." In this model God would make provision for the blessing to be received, but we must actually appropriate the blessing to derive any benefit from it. This model would be similar to our understanding of the blessing of salvation. Christ made provision for salvation through His life and work on the cross; but we are not saved until, by the grace of God, we appropriate the benefit of His work by faith unto ourselves. Thus, some people are saved and others are not. Some will know the blessing of salvation for an eternity, but others will not.

Ephesians 6:11 says to put on the whole armor of God. The armor is "of God"; our command is to "put on." This demonstrates God's provision and our appropriation of it. Then, God's intended purpose can be accomplished. Note that the appropriation is commanded.

Reject, Relinquish, Remove

By ordaining the family, the church, and civil government, God made provision for a three-freedom blessing: (1) personal and family; (2) religious; and (3) political. However, this was not freedom *from* something, or even *to* something, as much as it was freedom *for* something—a freedom to follow in an unconstrained manner God's purpose and plan. When we use God's provided freedom for His purpose, is when the benefit of the blessing is fully appropriated.

Perhaps we do not need to be as concerned about the blessing being removed, in terms of something that would be an act of a sovereign God, but that we have willfully rejected and relinquished the benefit of the blessing which God is still fully prepared for us to have. The rejection and relinquishment of the appropriation of this blessing is the area on which we need to focus. We will see that the benefits of God's blessing are easier kept than recaptured, once lost.

The threefold provision for blessing still exists in our country today: personal and family, political, and religious. The evidence that we are losing freedom in any of these areas to act according to God's purpose and plan in an unconstrained manner suggests that we as a nation are rejecting and relinquishing the benefit of the blessings inherent within these God-ordained institutions.

When things have regressed so negatively in any area that we could not change it even if we tried, it means we have lost (squandered) God's blessing. For example, consider how difficult it would be to reverse the legalization of abortion in our country or reverse the ban on prayer in public schools. Although not an impossibility, it would be extremely unlikely, given the current social and political environment. Christians have failed to stand forcefully, united, unequivocally, and without ceasing in these areas when the issues were being resolved in the legal, political, and cultural landscape – i.e. Christians willfully relinquished the blessing when they failed to retain the freedom. Today's bleak situation is the consequence. But God bless those who were in the fight from the beginning and are still in the battle today. More help for these valiant souls would have made a difference—and still can.

Some would suggest that because of the rampant number of abortions performed in our nation, along with other social sins,

God should withdraw (and perhaps already has withdrawn) His blessing from America. The horror of abortion suggests that when we Christians declined to use the arenas of politics and policy in the manner for which they were biblically mandated, we rejected a blessing God intended for us to realize through the proper use of His creation of civil government. When we reject, or fail to appropriate, God's provision for blessing, then we should not be surprised when unbiblical and anti-Christian government actions prevail, and the anti-blessing (a curse) then emerges.

The Blessing: What Or Who?

Of the three institutions God created, the civil government is structurally the most powerful. As such, one of its key duties is to protect the freedoms of God's other two institutions—the family and the church. But if civil government is not committed to biblical principles and Judeo-Christian values in its legislative, judicial, and administrative areas, then it will lack the desire or understanding required to protect them.

Then, it follows that the only way to ensure that the family and the church have the freedom to appropriate the blessing for which God has made provision is to have a civil government that fully reflects biblical principles and Judeo-Christian values. The only way to accomplish this is by having Christians' full participation in the political process to the degree that God provides the opportunity.

Now, this is the key that we must understand with respect to God's blessing for America: The active, informed, involved, engaged Christian is God's blessing to America. WE ARE the BLESSING!

It is the Christian citizen, from the foundation of our country, who insisted that God's institutions function in a manner that reflected biblical principles and Judeo-Christian values. What we characterize as God's blessing on America turns out to actually be God's blessing within it: the Christians were (and still are) the blessing! The most distinctive element that has been responsible for the special success of America as a nation is the Christian influence throughout the vital parts of its society.

Also, Regardless of how much we love our own country, we can praise God that this same blessing is available to any nation. If America wants to export freedom and democratic institutions around the world, we need to send missionaries—not emissaries and armies. Of course, the civil government can't send Christian missionaries, but a robust church can and will continue to do so. Nevertheless, the robustness of the church still significantly depends on the social and civil environment in which it exists.

So, we can help all countries by making our own nation a productive environment for the Christian church to flourish. We may or may not be called to serve as missionaries, but we are still assigned the role of the Great Commission Citizen in our own nation. In turn, we can ultimately bless all nations by sending missionaries.

The provision for the blessing was established when God created the institutions of the family, church, and civil government. In America, this blessing was appropriated when this nation was founded on Judeo-Christian values that were consistent with godly principles and these values and principles permeated all three institutions. These three institutions worked basically in harmony with each other, understanding God's purpose and recognizing His delegated authority for each. The blessing was activated when a political structure was established that provided the opportunity for Christians to pursue God's purpose and plan in a relatively unconstrained manner.

Unclogging the Conduit

Christians form the sole conduit by which God blesses America because the blessing only comes when Christian values are present—influencing, shaping, and directing God's ordained institutions.

> *Assuredly, I say to you, whatever you bind on earth will be bound in heaven, and whatever you loose on earth will be loosed in heaven.*
>
> *(Matt. 18:18 NKJV)*

We often sing "America" ("My Country, 'Tis of Thee"), "God Bless

America," "America the Beautiful," and "The Star-Spangled Banner." All these patriotic songs actually either are prayers, or contain prayers, and most of them are found in our hymnals. Moreover, we lift up countless prayers invoking God's blessing on our country. We truly want God to loose heaven's storehouse of blessing and pour it out upon our nation.

It seems, however, that we have bound on earth that which we want loosed in heaven. We have not spent the time, energy, effort, and expense as a Christian community to bless our nation by giving it what it most desperately needs: Christian involvement and impact in public policy and civil government.

Active, engaged Christians are God's blessing to America, but we have bound ourselves. Certainly we have been, and still are, a blessed nation because of our rich Christian heritage. However, much of the remnant of Christian influence we still have today has resulted simply because of social inertia from the past, and it will eventually grind to a halt if the current generation does not reenergize and reengage. Our patently anti-Christian culture degrades individuals, shows open hostility toward the family and the church, and opposes God's truth. These negative elements seem to be growing bolder and more successful each day.

We all pray for God to bless our country because we know it's needed. Surely, then, we will be willing to open ourselves to become the conduit of the blessing that God desires and for which we pray.

How have we bound ourselves here on earth and restrained God's fresh and full blessing for our country? Even though God has made it part of our duty, we have abandoned the domain of public policy and politics by a tradition of non-involvement, personal uncertainty, lack of knowledge, and anxiety about being too young, too old, too busy, or too ill-informed. Perhaps we also have been misguided by misinformation, as well as disinformation, with respect to the legitimate Christian role in our political process.

It is time to cast off that which blinds and that which binds and "loose on earth" our blessing on our country, and thereby advance the cause of Christ and His Great Commission. We need to choose to be God's blessing to America, as only we can, by fully engaging in public policy and the political process, thereby bringing biblical principles and Judeo-Christian values to the God-ordained, Christ-created institution of civil government.

SIX

Cautions and Encouragements

For the one who sows to his own flesh shall from the flesh reap corruption, but the one who sows to the Spirit will from the Spirit reap eternal life.

(*Gal. 6:8 NASB*)

The Greater Sin

Most Bible students would recognize Proverbs 14:34 (NASB), "Righteousness exalts a nation, but sin is disgrace to any people" and Proverbs 29:2, which says, "When the righteous increase, the people rejoice, but when a wicked man rules, people groan." These verses present a clear message about how entire nations are affected by the personal attitudes and actions regarding godly righteousness that national leaders bring to public office.

But how many people understand that when leaders rule unrighteously, not only must the leaders be accountable to God for their actions, but the citizens whose participation in the process brings about the unrighteous rule are also held responsible? Perhaps they are even *more* responsible if their knowledge of righteousness is greater.

In the events recorded in John 19:10-11, which we previously reviewed, Jesus was brought before Pilate in the infamous mock trial that would shortly lead to a sentence of death by crucifixion for our

Lord. The most heinous act ever surely must have been the worse sin ever. Not quite, according to John 19:11. Let's look at the verses again.

> *Pilate therefore said to Him, 'You do not speak to me? Do You not know that I have authority to release You, and I have authority to crucify You?' Jesus answered, 'You would have no authority over Me, unless it had been given you from above; for this reason he who delivered Me to you has the greater sin.'*

> *(John 19:10-11 NASB)*

Certainly what Pilate did was a sin, but according to Jesus' own words there was within this shameful process an even greater sin: ".... He who delivered Me to you has the greater sin" (John 19:11b). Who is this "he" that delivered Jesus to Pilate, and what is the greater sin?

Scholars disagree about whom Jesus was referring to as "he" in John 19:11b. Some say it was Judas (the betraying disciple); others say Caiaphas, the Jewish high priest at the time. Still others believe it was Annas, the father-in-law of Caiaphas and the person to whom Jesus was first brought after His arrest, while some say the Sanhedrin (the Jewish supreme council). Some say it must have been an individual because Jesus used the singular "he"; but others disagree, saying that the use of the singular "he" does not preclude a reference to multiple individuals, each being individually guilty (John 8:7).

The larger question with respect to the topic of this book is the second one: What is the "greater sin?" The greater sin is delegating the trial of Jesus to Pilate, knowing full well that the result would be the ultimate execution of an innocent Jesus. Luke 22:2 says, "And the chief priests and scribes sought how they might kill him, for they feared the people."

The Jewish spiritual and political leaders brought Jesus to Pilate to achieve an execution order. These members of the Sanhedrin had the scriptural writings (the law and the prophets). They had the history and tradition of the Jewish faith. They had the knowledge of the prophecies regarding the Messiah. They had first-hand knowledge of the life and work of Jesus. They had the greater sin because they had the greater knowledge. In other words, they had *sufficient* knowledge to know better.

This is the application: Just because we delegate decisions to governmental officials via elections (or apathy), we can never wash our hands of the ultimate responsibility. We will be held, in God's view, responsible for the actions that our elected representatives undertake, particularly with respect to God's righteousness. This is especially true if we knew or could have known in advance that the official would govern from an unbiblical perspective. Certainly, if we had knowledge of God's truth regarding the matter on which the official made unbiblical choices and supported him or her anyway, then He will, indeed, hold us responsible. When the wicked rule, we are responsible to the degree that we had a part in bringing it about. If we had knowledge enough and opportunity enough to act differently in our support of candidates, or used our participation in the political process to advance the election of candidates who would support ungodly laws, then we are culpable. We are culpable in God's view to the extent that we could actually have a greater sin than the offending public official. That is the clear message contained in the latter part of John 19:11.

For example, if we vote for a candidate, knowing that he or she supports abortion, then (1) certainly those participating in the abortions carry the responsibility for their involvement; (2) candidates and elected officials bear the responsibility to the degree that they permitted, encouraged, validated, or failed to aggressively attempt to stop abortion; and (3) the citizens with the right to vote hold the responsibility for their action or inaction that resulted in any pro-abortion candidate becoming a pro-abortion elected official. All involved anywhere in the process have sufficient knowledge of God's truth regarding abortion and will be held accountable by Him, but Christians may well be held to even a higher standard because of their greater knowledge.

A Christian knowledgeable about the ungodly evil of abortion who protects and enables the abortion industry by supporting known pro-choice (pro-abortion) politicians may have committed a greater sin in God's eyes than a frightened, vulnerable, manipulated young woman who yields to the pressure of having an abortion. John 19:11b gives a very extraordinarily stern warning to us today about attempting to politically pass the buck!

God will hold every political leader responsible for his or her actions, but God—as we are warned in John 19:11b—also looks past the political leader back to the people who enabled his or her unrighteous action. We cannot sit back in apathy and allow a political candidate, clearly opposed to godly standards, to be successful without our aggressive opposition. A sin worse than the ordering of Jesus' crucifixion is hard for us to imagine. If it had not been for what Jesus said in John 19:11b, we would have a hard time conceiving such a thing.

In a form of government where public officials are democratically elected, the principle of John 19:11b places an awesome responsibility upon the Christian, who has been given knowledge of God's righteous standards, to do everything to assure that in an election process, those who pledge to honor godly standards will be upheld and those who pledge to violate those standards will be defeated. That is a principle that can never be violated.

As Christians, we have the greater knowledge of God's righteousness because we not only have the Bible, but we also have the Holy Spirit, who enlivens our understanding of God's Word and brings us under conviction regarding our motivations and actions. Thus, we are extraordinarily responsible for using our ability to participate in public policy, civil government and the political process to ensure that this God-ordained institution of civil government reflects biblical principles and Judeo-Christian values.

We must only support those candidates for public office whom we know for certain will be good stewards of godly values. We can only support public policy that incorporates and reflects godly values. We can only accomplish this by being active in the political process.

As King Jehoshaphat was told by a messenger from God regarding his unholy political alliance:

> Should you help the ungodly and love those who hate the Lord? Because of this, wrath has gone out against you from the Lord.

The Political Imperative

(2 Chron. 19:2b AB)

In the New Testament, the apostle Paul also instructs,

*Do not be yoked together with unbelievers. For what do righteous-
ness and wickedness have in common? Or what fellowship can light
have with darkness?*

(2 Cor. 6:14 NIV)

The Gates of Hell

*. . I will build my church, and the gates of hell shall not prevail
against it.*

(Matt. 16:18b KJV)

In this verse, there is no question about Jesus' reference to His
church, although there is some debate about whether the word translated "hell" in the King James Version is better translated "Hades."
The accompanying question is whether the use of the term "hell"
or "Hades" makes a difference in the overall interpretation of the
verse. Regardless, hell is a real place, according to the Bible.

The reference to "gates" may or may not be metaphorical, but
the idea serves a purpose here. What do the "gates of hell" represent? One of the features of the gates of hell is that inside them, no
element of God exists. Some biblical information exists regarding
the nature of hell, but the descriptions are only a hint of the real
horror. But one thing is for sure: God is absent.

But where are the gates of hell today, in the church age? In a
practical sense, the gates of hell exist wherever the world system
puts up a blockade and says to Christians, "Stop! Keep Out! No
Christianity Allowed! Violators will be at minimum prosecuted,
and probably persecuted!"

Today the gates of hell are being built at the front doors of the
public school system, universities, the news and entertainment media centers, the business community, the legislative halls, and the
judicial system. These institutions set the agenda for our culture.
Here, Satan's operatives or clueless accomplices have said, "Nothing
Christian Allowed Here—No Exceptions." And they seem to be getting their way, which negatively affects our families, our churches,

and ultimately the Great Commission.

Is the church today prevailing against these gates? Pacification, appeasement, accommodation, isolation, and cocooning are all techniques individuals and groups have used to try to live free from any conflict with evil. But these don't really work as long-term options.

We won't prevail against "the gates of hell" while locked in our homes. Moreover, through television, the Internet, and other methods, Satan is penetrating the confines of our home (at our invitation, I might add). The Enemy, in absence of any resistance, just moves those gates closer and closer. Our only hope is to stand up, step out, and contend for the faith.

Thou Shall Not Tempt the Lord thy God

Then the devil taketh him up into the holy city, and setteth him on a pinnacle of the temple, and saith unto him, If thou be the Son of God, cast thyself down: for it is written, He shall give his angels charge concerning thee: and in their hands they shall bear thee up, lest at any time thou dash thy foot against a stone. Jesus said unto him, It is written again, Thou shalt not tempt the Lord thy God.

(Matt. 4:5-7 KJV)

After His baptism, Jesus fasted for forty days in the wilderness. Following this period, Jesus was tempted by the Devil. Three specific temptations are recorded in the Book of Matthew.

In the incident described in this particular passage, Jesus was being tempted to prove, for all Jerusalem to see, that He was the Son of God by demonstrating that God would protect Him. Satan suggested that Jesus accomplish this feat by jumping off the top of the temple so that God would rescue Him. Satan even used the words of Psalm 91:11-12 to justify his specious argument. Jesus, of course, rejected this ploy, quoting the Scriptures to back up His position. Jesus' response was, "Thou shalt not tempt the Lord thy God" (Deut. 6:16 KJV).

When we willfully get ourselves into an impossible situation, and then tell God it is His job to bail us out, while trying to use the Scriptures to justify our presumption, then we are tempting God.

As Jesus responded to the Devil, this is a forbidden practice. It is similar to the familiar verse, "Shall we continue in sin, that grace may abound?" (Rom. 6:1 KJV). The answer was a clear, "God forbid!" And God does forbid this.

If we have neglected our opportunity, duty, and sacred trust regarding our role in the political process and our country suffers as a result, and then we woefully quote 2 Chronicles 7:14, calling on God to "heal our land," we must ask, "Are we not tempting God?" The answer is, "Yes, we are." Shall we ask God do things for us that He has, in fact, assigned to us? Furthermore, should we then put God's reputation on the line to produce results, when this was actually our job all along?

When we are not willing to do that which we can do, are supposed to do, and God has assigned us to do, subsequently getting ourselves and our country into extreme difficulty, and then quote a Scripture back to God, invoking Him to do our job for us and bail us out, we are tempting God. Although God is gracious and merciful, we should never presume upon those attributes.

If we assess the negative impact our culture has on our families, our churches, and the Great Commission and then proceed to quote 2 Chronicles 7:14 as we pray for God to heal our land, then we must realize that simply by appropriating the opportunity that He has already graciously given us in this country, we can answer this prayer beyond all our expectations. Surely, as Christians, we will not pray to God to heal our land, and then reject His answer to our prayer when it means that God intends to "heal our land" with our own hands—by using us to engage the culture through the political process.

If My People

If my people, which are called by my name, shall humble themselves, and pray, and seek my face, and turn from their wicked ways; then will I hear from heaven, and will forgive their sin, and will heal their land.

(2 Chron. 7:14 KJV)

This is my interpretation of 2 Chronicles 7:14 as it applies to the time and topic of today: *"If. . .".* This is a very highly conditional verse. We need to fully understand the terms and conditions set forth. There will be no fulfillment of the promise of this verse unless God's pre-conditions are met. Even more than one might suspect at the outset, there is a special reason for this.

> *". . . my people, . . ."* "My people," in this church age, refers to Christians. These aren't the ones who merely claim the name of Christ, but those He knows are actually His.

> *". . . which are called by my name, . . ."* Set aside the name you call yourself for one moment. What do others call you? God is looking for those who aren't ashamed to bear the name "Christian" and be known as "Christian" in every area of their lives.

That means, among other things, that one should seamlessly apply the same set of biblical principles and Judeo-Christian values to one's private life, personal life, family life, work life, school life, social life, church life, public life, and civic life. An implied boldness on our part is required to reach that place where we are called by His name—not just by ourselves, but by others.

Are you called by His name in the venue of the political process? Would you be readily identified as a "values voter," "conservative Christian," or member of the "religious right"? Or, if accused, would you recoil from those names like Peter did at the trial of Jesus?

It is one thing to be called by His name for identity purposes, but sometimes another to be called (compelled) by His name into action. Even Christians who are engaged in political and civic activity enter into that arena for quite a variety of purposes: taxes, Second Amendment issues, Tenth Amendment issues, etc. All of these may be worthy issues, but 2 Chronicles 7:14 suggests that God is seeking to work through those who are called (compelled) into action by His name—that is, to accomplish the issues through civil government that God intends to be achieved by this institution. Even as Christians, it seems of little use to quote and pray 2 Chronicles 7:14 if our purpose and practice in the civil arena is not aligned with the One to whom we pray to intercede. Our motivation *does* matter to God.

". . .shall humble themselves . . ." Humility is the opposite of pride. God requires something from us that involves setting aside our pride, our prejudices, preferences, and our traditions, if necessary, to follow His leading. According to this verse, this is a non-negotiable pre-condition.

". . .and pray . . ." God answers prayer according to His sovereign will. However, one of the key functions of prayer is to conform our will to God's will, not vice versa.

This verse says, "pray," but it does not say precisely what to pray. One might think that the prayer would be for God to heal our land, but He has already promised to do this if we just fulfill His pre-conditions. So the proper prayer here must be about "His people" (meaning all His people) fulfilling all the conditions that God requires so the land will be healed as He promised.

Sometimes we pray for God to give us a particular desired result, but His only answer is to show us the route we must follow to achieve the result. When we or someone we know experiences a serious illness, for example, we pray for a healing from God. God, in His sovereignty, may heal instantaneously. On the other hand, God may open the door to a divinely ordered process in order to achieve the cure we seek, which may involve doctors, medicines, technology, and time—along with our commitment, discipline, and perseverance.

When we pray for the healing of our land, we desire an immediate result, but God's answer is a route. We want a *product*, which is a healed land. Instead, God gives us a *process* for the healing of the land. Our society is so dynamic that any status quo is only short lived without constant maintenance. Our land needs more than a quick fix; if that was all we got, then it would not be long before we are right back in a mess again. We need a process that works as long as we will work the process. We need a divinely ordered solution that is suitable for the long term—a course of action that can be successfully applied continuously, generation to generation, and that can transcend time, geography, nationalities, and cultures. We need a universally applicable and sustainable solution. Praise the Lord! That is exactly what God gives us.

> *". . .and seek my face. . ."* Getting face to face with God means clearly receiving His message and instructions without any filters, interference, or excuses. It first involves humility — a willingness to set aside any of our own pre-conditions we might want to cling to. It involves a true desire to conform our will to His will achieved through prayer. This, then, is the prayer we should pray—that we would be worthy vessels to receive God's Word, face to face, in the way and for the purpose that He intended. We must ask God to help us set aside our preferences, preconceived opinions, or presumptions and be unconditionally obedient to the message we receive from Him. Since the final objective of the verse is the healing of the land, then the conforming of our will to God's message is going to relate to that goal. This could require a lot of humility and some really honest "face time" if the message from God calls us to do something contrary to what we have believed, practiced, and perhaps taught up to this point.

> *". . .and turn from their wicked ways. . ."* Turning from biblically wicked ways should be considered synonymous with the act of repentance. Repentance involves willfully turning away from the wrong way, and making the choice to turn toward the godly way—not turning begrudgingly, but having once rejected God's way, now eagerly desiring to learn of and follow God's way. The turning from a "wicked way" mentioned in this verse must mean turning the exact opposite way from the current path. This is not like a child who is forced to do chores and responds with no heart, but rather like a person who has made a great discovery and now eagerly seeks the benefit.

The Bible teaches that the way of the world is a wicked one. The word translated "wicked" in 2 Chronicles 7:14 verse means—among other things— distress, misery, injury, calamity, and adversity. So the way of the world ultimately leads to adversity, distress and calamity. When Christian participation in public policy, civil government, and the political process is based on the same motivation as the secular world, then we walk with the world. This certainly can't be counted on to help the Christian family, the church, and the Great Commission, and is just as likely to have a negative effect. Examples of political participation according to the ways of the world which may not immediately occur to us include voting one's traditional political party or voting one's pocketbook, or even voting for a friend for public office when any of these examples involve supporting a person who is not personally living by, and not fully committed to governing by biblical principles. Please note that certainly none of these identified activities are wrong unless and until they entail supporting a violation of biblical principles and Judeo-Christian values.

When we repent of these acts, and then willfully and eagerly turn toward carrying out the Christian role of the Great Commission citizen and the political imperative, we will finally be on the right route.

> *"...then will I hear from heaven..."* There are many positions for praying discussed in the Bible, including standing, sitting, kneeling, and lying prostrate before God. The Bible doesn't mention a prayer position in which an individual turns his back on God and then prays back over his shoulder while wishing for the best. That is why the repenting (turning) precedes the hearing. God's "hearing" does not simply mean an awareness of thoughts or words; it refers to an acceptance of the petition to be answered according to His sovereign will.

First, we must get our mind right (seek God's face), and then we need to get our heart right (turn from our wicked ways). Then at last we will be in a position to point the remainder of our self in the right direction, which begins the answer to the promise of this scripture.

> *"...and will forgive their sin..."* Notice that this phrase doesn't mention "sins," but a "sin," because it is a specific sin that stands between the people and the healing of the land.

Inherent within the concept of forgiveness is the term "release." When God forgives a sin, He graciously releases us from the just punishment that is due to us because we've committed that sin. As Christians, we understand that this is possible because Jesus has already paid the penalty and borne the punishment for our sins on the cross. In this case, when we humbly turn to God with an overriding desire to conform our will to His will for us, and then honestly receive His message while committing to obey it without reservation, then we, with God's help, will begin to be released from the bondage and confusion that had caused us to sin. Always true to His Word, God frees us from His just punishment for our sin (even though we may have to live with some negative consequences of our prior actions). We are now prepared to follow God's plan for us. With all His pre-conditions being specifically and sincerely met, God promises to forgo the judgment we deserve, and in its place accomplish the healing of the land promised in this passage.

> *"...and will heal their land..."* The healing of our nation will not come through some mysterious, independent act of God that we stand by in awe and observe. Indeed, if that is our expectation we may have to wait a long time for this healing. In fact, we have been quoting and praying 2 Chronicles 7:14 for a long time now, and things only seem to be getting worse. Nevertheless, the healing will come when and because God's people become conformed to His will regarding the manner in which they act toward the God-created, God-ordained institution of civil government.

We have to desire the healing badly enough to humble ourselves, even to the point of confessing that we are the problem. After all, if the healing of the land is pre-conditioned for certain things Christians must do, then our corresponding lack must be the problem. That is extraordinarily encouraging because it means that we do not need to be discouraged or defeated by those who oppose biblical principles and Judeo-Christian values. Others are not in control of how things work out—by God's plan we are. Others are in control only to the degree that we surrender control to them. There is nothing biblical about surrendering one of God's institutions to the enemy. God desires for our land to be healed. God's plan is to heal our land with our hands.

So Close, Yet So Far

There is an old "church joke" that goes something like this: The local congregation is trying to raise money for a special project, perhaps a building program. The pastor announces that there's some good news and some bad news. "The good news," says the pastor, "is that God has provided all the money we need for our project." The pastor continues, "But the bad news is that the money is still in your pocket." So close, yet so far.

That story is analogous to much that is occurring in our own country today. The family, the church, and the Great Commission are being negatively affected because the civil government is not operating in accordance with the manner that God designed. The government is not fulfilling its God-ordained role, and thus cannot serve its God-ordained purpose.

The good news is that God has provided us with the solution to that problem. The bad news is that the solution is us, and we collectively are not yet doing an acceptable job in fulfilling the obligation that God has placed upon us. Even though we are sitting on a great opportunity, we are failing to sufficiently act on that opportunity. We are so close, yet so far.

Proverbs 19:24 (NASB) says, "The sluggard buries his hand in the dish, but will not even bring it back to his mouth." We are not told anything else in this passage, but it is not hard to figure out how things will end: if this sad figure never gets around to getting the food to his mouth, he dies. He has everything he needs to survive right there in his hands, but he won't appropriate it to his benefit.

Make no mistake about the message here. The Christian pastors, leaders, and members who are carrying out God's cause today are not sluggards—in fact, quite the opposite. There are many, many tireless workers who are true champions for Christ, working from sunup to sundown and well beyond that.

But collectively, we Christians in America (with some wonderful exceptions) have been slow to respond to our duty in one critical arena. Our cumulative response in this area has been sluggardly: not because our commitment to Christ lacks fervor, but because our understanding in this specific area has been deficient.

Still, this example from Proverbs seems like an all–too–close-to-reality example of Christianity in our country today with respect to political activity. Because of our form of government, we have the freedom, the opportunity, and the ability to make a difference in our society, government, and community. Because the government was given to us by God through our forefathers, we now hold it in our hands. Let us not be the generation of Christians apparently willing to die with the opportunity in our grasp, but unwilling to ever get around to doing anything with it.

There are plenty of Christian workers available to make all the difference; it is not the overworking of the overworked church worker that is called for here. Instead, it involves the teaching, training, and engaging of those Christians whom God has called to participate in this mission, this special ministry to the arenas dealing with public policy, civil government, and the political process. Just like with other areas that serve God's purpose, it is the job of the church to also nurture, encourage, and provide a gateway for this mission. That must come first.

Tradition

A special word needs to be said about the topic of tradition, regarding the role it plays in the political process. In politics, as with many other areas, tradition most often takes root when a useful, beneficial practice is repeated over an extended period of time.

Eventually, however, conditions inevitably change. We must ask ourselves these questions: Is this tradition still useful? Is it harmful to us now? Does it make any difference at all? Not all traditions are bad just because times have changed; in fact, some still serve a very useful purpose. But all of our traditions need to be reassessed from time to time. However, the very nature of traditions means that they don't get re-evaluated very often. We tend to put our traditions on automatic pilot; that is usually what makes them traditions.

As Christians, we have a direct duty from God to establish biblical standards in civil government. Thus, just as for any action we take, we must re-evaluate our traditions in this area to ensure that they are consistent with our assignment from God to become Great Commission Citizens.

Is it possible for our traditions to conflict with our duty? Jesus warns us that this can indeed happen.

> *Jesus replied, And why do you break the command of God for the sake of your tradition? For God said, 'Honor your father and mother' and 'Anyone who curses his father or mother must be put to death.' But you say that if a man says to his father or mother, 'Whatever help you might otherwise have received from me is a gift devoted to God,' he is not to 'honor his father' with it. Thus you nullify the word of God for the sake of your tradition. You hypocrites! Isaiah was right when he prophesied about you:*
>
> *'These people honor me with their lips, but their hearts are far from me. They worship me in vain; their teachings are but rules taught by men.'*

(Matt. 15:3-9 NIV)

Jesus was speaking to "some Pharisees and teachers of the law" in this passage. Those leaders represented the cultural, civil, and spiritual leadership of the day, but they were ignoring their moral and scriptural duty.

The Pharisees should have been assisting their parents with direct financial support when they needed it. Instead, they had invented a reason to ignore this scriptural mandate and deliberately misinterpreted the Scriptures for their own financial benefit. They played religious but lived secular. In politics, this is called "voting your pocketbook." These religious "giants" were not willing to make a personal sacrifice, even when confronted with clear spiritual requirements. According to Jesus, the fault was with their unworthy tradition.

We know that traditions abound in the area of politics. Some individuals have traditions of voting in a certain manner which, in all honesty, is in conflict with the call to be a Great Commission Citizen. We must re-examine those traditions in light of our requirements to promote biblical principles and Judeo-Christian values in government.

Some local churches have a tradition of downplaying and ignoring the importance of civil government and the political process. This is a tradition which, as we have seen, is not consistent with our

God-given political imperative. We must re-evaluate that stand, and then take corrective action.

The result of maintaining these false traditions is the election of people to office who are not committed first and foremost to applying biblical principles and the Judeo-Christian value system to the civil government and judicial system. The result is damage to the Christian family and the Great Commission.

In all of these matters, we must stand under the truth and guidance of the Scriptures. The Pharisees and teachers of the law in Jesus' day were ignoring clear biblical principles in favor of their tradition. They didn't get away with it, however; instead, they received Jesus' stern condemnation. Thankfully, as Bible-honoring Christians, once we understand God's truth presented in the Scriptures, we will follow it explicitly and faithfully, and will not let past traditions be a stumbling block for today's mission.

> *Beware lest any man spoil you through philosophy and vain deceit, after the tradition of men, after the rudiments of the world, and not after Christ.*
>
> *(Col. 2:8 KJV)*

SEVEN

Inexorably Interconnected

What therefore God hath joined together, let not man put asunder.

(Mark 10:9 KJV)

Theologically Interconnected

As Christians, we must not attempt to live our lives as if we can separate and disconnect that which by God's design is intentionally and inescapably linked. We do not, cannot, and were never intended to live in complete isolation from the world. Our constant challenge is to be "in the world, but not of the world" (John 17:15; Rom. 12:2). We are inexorably interconnected with what goes on around us. The political system affects the culture, and the culture constantly tries to shape our morals and our perspective on moral issues, which, in turn, affects how we view our participation in politics. The tone and tenor of the political system affects how political participation is viewed as a proper topic for the church. The attitude of the church toward politics influences the way Christians participate. The degree of Christian participation affects the manner in how politics is translated into the culture. Politics and the culture, for better or worse, have a huge effect on the family, the church, and the Great

Commission. And so it goes.

First, society inherently incorporates and reflects some dominate moral view. The Bible sets forth a particular moral and ethical view that we refer to as the Judeo-Christian value system. As we surely understand by now, because we are Christians, we must be unequivocally committed to this biblically based moral standard— totally, absolutely, at all times, and under all circumstances. We can all agree with that.

The accompanying truth is that God's three institutions (the family, church, and civil government) can only successfully provide the full blessing and benefit that God intended when they fully reflect the biblical principles that apply to them. Obviously, committed, Bible-honoring Christians are in the best position to guide those institutions.

The more the biblical standards gets distorted, the greater the negative impingement on each institution to which they were intended to apply. Sooner or later, the harmful effects reach the point of severely and negatively affecting the advancement of the family, the church, the nation, and the Great Commission. This becomes extraordinarily critical to us as Christians since carrying out the Great Commission is our singular overriding purpose.

Remember that the core of the Great Commission involves the family, the church, and civil government. Each has to operate according to God's design, employ God's delegated authority, function within its God-designated boundaries and reflect the biblical principles and Judeo-Christian values that undergird all of God's creation.

Churches can become unbalanced when they try to command the family and usurp the role of the parents, especially the father. Churches should undergird the individual family unit, not try to dominate it. Governments also become unbalanced when they try to usurp the role of the family and undermine the church. Moreover, families are negatively affected when they live apart from God and the church while behaving toward the government as if it were some sort of "secular god."

Our worldview makes a difference on how we view the role of

politics. We are immersed and interconnected to the civil and political systems to the point that we cannot avoid them, nor, by God's design, were we ever intended to. Attempting to disconnect is denial; retreat equals defeat. No rational Christian voluntarily hands over to the Enemy one of God's precious and powerful institutions to be used against him, his family, and his church.

No man can serve two masters, and you will serve the government. Because the government is more powerful than you, it will make you serve it. The only way not to be torn between God and the government occurs when government fulfills its proper role, consistent with biblical principles and Judeo-Christian values. That can only happen when you, as a well-informed Christian, are fully participating in the full range of political opportunities available to you.

Politically Interconnected

One of the primary reasons that God created civil government was to establish social order. Of course, officials who have control of civil government may or may not use its power and structure for the role and purpose that God intended. God will require them to give an account of their action, whether they're good or evil. Yet, because of our form of government, God will ultimately hold us responsible for the way we hold these government officials accountable because it is our job to be stewards of this God-ordained institution through those whom we elect. Furthermore, it is our responsibility to supervise these elected officials after the election as well.

Because we are the primary holders of civil authority, those whom we elect as our representatives serve at our pleasure. The institution of government may have authority over us, and the political offices (e.g. governor, senator, etc.) may be due our respect; but the individuals whom we elect to be our representatives to operate the government are our servants. They should never forget that, but more important, we should never forget that either. It is a paradox of sorts: We are subject to the institution of civil government and its offices that are over us. At the same time, however, these politicians are subject to us because they only hold the offices of government by our collective pleasure. In our political system we are both responsible to and responsible for government.

That is why we should only be electing those who have convinced us that they have both the desire and ability to see that all aspects of government are conducted in a manner that incorporates biblical principles and the Judeo-Christian value system. Since candidates are elected to office by majority vote, then a Christian eligible to register and vote is never "off the hook" regarding responsibility in this area.

In our representative form of government, those who hold the offices must first be democratically elected by the individual citizens. This places an awesome responsibility upon us as Christians, who have been given knowledge of God's righteous standards. We must do everything to ensure that in an election process, those who have pledged to honor godly standards will be upheld, and those undertaking to violate those standards will be defeated. This must be our commitment regardless of any other considerations.

There may be many things to consider in choosing which candidates we will support. Nevertheless, no considerations override the requirement of a candidate's uncompromising allegiance to biblical principles and Judeo-Christian values.

Critically, biblically-based civil government is needed to counter the threat that stems from situations and circumstances which would create such disorder in the civil arena, even to the point of anarchy.

Anarchy occurs when neither the institutions that provide the reliable stability needed for civil order, nor the mores that guide society, are functioning in the necessary manner or degree to ensure a sustainable society. The result is that society begins to destabilize and disintegrate into chaos.

Some threats are so damaging to civil order that they can go beyond general social decay and actually serve as gateways to anarchy. These are areas that we especially need to be on guard against. Following are some examples:

1. *Moral relativism* (Legalization of drugs, toleration of

corrupt government officials, abortion, and same-sex marriage fit into this category.) In the end, moral relativism is an untenable societal model.

2. *Misjudging or living in denial about the basic nature of the human race, especially as it relates to evil and aggression* (e.g. believing that passivity and appeasement are plausible solutions to dealing with evil such as crime, terrorism, and direct or indirect threats from hostile nations.) Believing that belligerent evil can be dealt with in any manner by a nation other than force and strength is an ultimately futile approach to dealing with evil, whether it is internal or external. It all goes back to the nature of fallen man and what resides deep in the heart of the human race. (Jer 17:9, Mt 15:19)

3. *Economic systems that have historically proved to be hopelessly dysfunctional and ultimately unsustainable.* (Socialism, economic fascism, government redistribution schemes, and government-managed economies are examples that fit into this category.) Such schemes always inefficiently produce unacceptable results at an excessive cost and are inherently unsuitable for anything but minimal levels of performance.

Moreover, a government that attempts to be godlike by doing everything for everyone is ultimately unsustainable. So, even good intentions can lead to negative consequences if we are not aware of the realities of human nature, and natural limitations and God-given boundaries with respect to government.

Whenever a government is promoting philosophies such as the above, a threatening instability exists. A general economic stagnation then leads to social unrest and then possible anarchy. In response, that which follows may be the aggressive (and even oppressive) reaction of civil government to attempt to control the instability while probably maintaining the very systems which have caused the problem.

The point of this discussion is not an attempt to be partisan or a "policy wonk" with respect to the detailed workings of civil government. Instead, the goal is for Christians to recognize that the basic approach the government takes toward ruling its citizenry makes a immeasurably huge difference. Once its central concepts are put into place and implemented through legislation and public policy, the results can have a deep influence and impact on the family, as well as the provision for Christians to fulfill the Great Commission.

It is extraordinarily hard to reverse unbiblical public policy once it is in place. Instead, it is much wiser to be able to recognize unbiblical policy in advance and then act to prevent it from ever becoming public policy. The family, the church, and the Great Commission function best in free, open, safe, biblically moral and economically sustainable societies. This kind of healthy growth requires a civil government based on biblical principles and Judeo-Christian values. Thus, we must look at the underlying political philosophies of candidates seeking office in that regard. That is one of the things a Great Commission Citizen does.

The first step on the path to building a successful civil government is to stay off the road(s) to disorder and anarchy. These roads are sometimes wide, appealing, and popular; and bounded on each side with positive platitudes, good intentions, and "happily ever after" promises. But if they call on government to operate outside its God-designed role, build upon false assumptions about human nature, or pursue inherently unsustainable political or economic models, then disappointment, defeat, unrest, and even chaos and anarchy will follow. The Christian family, the church, and the Great Commission do not thrive under such conditions. It is the job of the Christian, exercising the full measure of opportunity available, to make sure that does not happen, and the job of the church to teach that truth.

If the foundations be destroyed, what can the righteous do?

Psalm 11:3 (KJV)

Culturally Interconnected

The list of issues (sins) that can negatively impact the family would be too long to deal with individually in this discussion. Countless sermons and many excellent ministries, books, and entire organizations are dedicated to this critical subject. Let's all be thankful for those dedicated to family ministries. But suffice it to say that if the institution of the family is held in mockery and disrepute from without or within, undermined instead of undergirded, then Christian families will increasingly be on the defensive—struggling instead of leading by example.

This will occur because, try as we may, the Christian family cannot separate itself from the enormous impact of the surrounding culture. When Christian families become too negatively influenced by the philosophies within the present world system, then the institution of the family as a whole can no longer serve as that fundamentally critical, safe, nurturing, secure, stable foundation for society.

Thus, the damaged family will not be that bastion of strength against the decline of the social structure and the civil society, making the society even more vulnerable to destabilization. This is why one of the primary acts of self-preservation by any civil government should involve the protection of the family. Conversely, one of the precursors to anarchy is the systematic weakening of the traditional, historical, and biblical model of the family.

The societal assault on the family today is two-fold. First, the culture is focusing its attack on the individual family members. Each one of us, as family members, has our own particular vulnerabilities in this regard, so we are well acquainted with this battle. There are ministries that spend every waking hour, as well as individuals who spend sleepless nights, over issues that negatively affect family members. Our prayers are with them.

The other attack is on the institution of the family itself. This assault is being spearheaded through the homosexual activists' efforts to render the biblical institution of the family void by attempting to socially, legislatively, and judicially redefine marriage under law to incorporate "same-sex marriage," or achieve the same objective through so-called "civil unions."

These attempts by homosexual activists and their allies hold God's created institution of marriage up to ridicule and, if successful, would render the term "marriage" meaningless for all of society. A review of the following passages will serve to enlighten or refresh anyone on God's view of homosexuality: Leviticus 18:22; Romans 1:18-31; 1 Corinthians 6:9-10; 1Timothy 1:10; Jude 1:7.

When these attacks on the family and biblical marriage are endorsed—and even instigated—by the government, then the institution of the family will ultimately be damaged. Because we are not isolated, this will eventually negatively impact the Christian family, which will result in a less focused and less vigorous church, since an inordinate amount of time, energy, and resources will be required to minister to the damaged Christian family. A weaker church will also be more vulnerable to unbiblical teaching and practices creeping inside its walls, further damaging the church and its individual church families. This becomes a downward trek that is more and more difficult to reverse.

Of course, Christians becoming involved in politics certainly will not somehow resolve all the problems that the Christian family faces today. However, because of the impact that civil government has on the society, and thus the individual and the family, Christians should be more than eager to fully incorporate all the tools God has provided to carry out His purpose.

Remember, also, that only a civil government reflecting biblical values and Judeo-Christian principles will have the desire and ability to protect the Christian family. That is why it is incumbent on every Christian to not only protect their individual family (which is one of the strengths of our current Christian culture), but also the institution of the family itself. This is to be done first and foremost by ensuring that the government is family friendly, which means that Christians must be extensively and effectively involved in public policy through the political process. Indeed, the fight over the institution of the family and the legal structure of marriage is primarily a political one.

An unswerving commitment to biblically based morality with regard to the family and in regard to the institution of marriage is the core of a stable society. The opposite position is the moral relativism that occurs when groups or individuals attempt to decide at any time what is right or wrong while rejecting the absolute authority of the Bible. That contrary pathway leads to social degradation and potentially a gateway to social chaos in which survival, not furthering the Great Commission, dominates within the Christian community.

Since it is part of the legitimate role of civil government to protect and not undermine the institution of the family and marriage, we must always make sure those we place in a position of responsibility in civil government demonstrate by their background, platform, performance, and political alliances that they are in complete concurrence with the biblical worldview regarding the family and marriage. Moreover, they must be willing to vigorously apply the influence of their office to champion and undergird these principles.

To put it more bluntly, we must never, never support any political candidate, political appointment, or political party that promotes or accommodates the anti-biblical position of same-sex marriage or civil unions. Also, since it is also the role of civil government to deliver justice that is consistent with biblical principles and Judeo-Christian values and not undermine them, then we must always make sure that those we place in positions of responsibility in the judicial system, as well as legislative and administrative, areas of our government show us that they completely agree with the biblical worldview, and will reflect these principles in the execution of the duties of their office.

Financially Interconnected

First Timothy 6:10, in the King James Version says "....the love of money is the root of all evil. . . ". The New King James Version says "all kinds of evil," and the NASB says, "all sorts of evil." The point is clear. Most of us are also familiar with the English historian Lord Acton, who authored the famous quote, "Power tends to corrupt, and absolute power corrupts absolutely."

A look back at history and at our world today, along with an honest look at our own country, would indicate that corruption in government has been and is rampant. Pervasive corruption matters because the government, economy, and society become substantially dysfunctional and grossly underperforming whenever there is government corruption. When the government is dysfunctional then Christian family is negatively affected, and the church and the Great Commission are as well.

In some countries, government and business corruption is so widespread and intertwined in the institutional fabric that the citizenry just accepts it as a matter of fact. A few elite groups prosper, but the masses don't. In the United States, we as a society still formally reject illegal corruption, but seem mostly indifferent to legalized corruption. Legalized corruption can take the form of quid pro quo campaign contributions, preferential tax breaks for special interest groups, endless pandering and favors by lobbyists, and vast funding of special pet projects; not to mention, an unwillingness of entrenched politicians to eliminate waste because it buys votes; selective enforcement of laws for political purposes, or countless other ways. Although, many of these are perhaps technically legal in structure, this kind of moral corruption abounds within politics today — and it is corruption, pure and simple.

And where the willingness to embrace "legalized" corruption exists, other unseen forms of unethical moral compromise and likely illegal corruption are surely also present in abundance, further rotting the core of civil government upon which we all depend for safety, security, stability, justice, fairness, and opportunity. Most of this corruption stems from the love of money or the power that money can buy.

Does all this seem hopeless? It is, except for one thing. There is no real way to get money completely out of politics; but there is an alternative to corruption, and it is Christianity. Even though Christians aren't perfect, the Holy Spirit is perfect and incorruptible. Christians have the gift of the Holy Spirit and are commanded to be filled and controlled by the Spirit (Rom. 8:9, Eph. 5:18).

As important as they may be, there are not enough laws, rules, regulations, watchdogs, disclosures, investigations, courts, or prisons to keep corruption at a level that does not negatively affect the society, economy, and therefore, the family. Besides, expecting corrupt government to police itself is an exercise in futility. Electing Christians to public offices who have consistently shown that they are yielded to the Holy Spirit in their lives will squeeze out corruption. This is an example of overcoming evil with good. By the way, a pro-abortion, pro-homosexual politician is not yielded to the Holy Spirit regardless of the Christian credentials they tout.

Yes, Christians will fail from time to time. Yes, there are non-Christians whose ethics protect them from falling into illegal corruption. No, not everyone who has ever received a campaign contribution is somehow hopelessly corrupt. But, the fact remains that the immense amount of money and other favors (both legal and illegal) flowing to and from the politicians, and the resultant increase in corruption in all its forms (both legal and illegal) is enormous and growing. Only the overwhelming presence of Christians engaged in the areas of public policy, civil government, and the political process can or will make the difference. By and large, only those fully committed to biblical principles and our Judeo-Christian value system will even want to make a difference. Most politicians don't want to make a difference; they just want their turn at the feeding trough, and, of course, get re-elected.

The only thing that will get Christians to participate in the political process in sufficient numbers to make the required difference is the insistence of local churches for their members to get involved. Churches must preach, teach, encourage, promote, and practice the principles of the political imperative and the Great Commission Citizen. That is the only cure for the insidious rot of corruption. As Christians, we must face the fact that it is not just that we have the only cure, but we are the only cure to this disease.

Philippians 4:8 (KJV) says,

...whatsoever things are true, whatsoever things are honest,

whatsoever things are just, whatsoever things are pure, whatsoever things are lovely, whatsoever things are of good report; if there be any virtue, and if there be any praise, think on these things.

Remember, one of the key functions of government is providing a framework where good things can happen. Several of the items in this verse from Philippians apply directly to the administration of civil government (i.e. truth, honesty, and justice).

Proverbs 16:11 (NKJV) says, "Honest weights and scales are the Lord's; all the weights in the bag are His work." Expressing the same concept from the opposite view, Proverbs 20:10 (NASB) says, "Differing weights and differing measures, both of them are abominable to the LORD." The fundamental principle behind the concept of "justice" under biblical standards involves individuals, through the administration of government, getting what they deserve, and conversely, not getting what they don't deserve.

It is our responsibility to see that those applicable values listed in Philippians and Proverbs, and numerous other passages throughout the Bible, are reflected in the areas for which we have responsibility—not only self, family, work, and church, but also government. Corruption cannot coexist with biblical values and vise versa.

Depart In Peace, Be Ye Warmed and Filled

Stories about the "unsinkable" *Titanic*, the luxury ocean liner, are legend, but you haven't heard my version yet. Let's revise and replay the story. In my version the owner of the *Titanic* is on its maiden voyage. In reality, *Titanic* owner U. S. industrialist John Pierpont Morgan did not make that voyage. But in my story, the owner is on board and has as his guest a world-class ship captain. Even though this guest isn't the captain of the *Titanic,* he is still a fully capable ship captain who happens to be taking the voyage because he's a friend of the owner.

The owner and his friend, standing on the deck of the *Titanic,* clearly see that the ship is headed toward a massive iceberg field. Unless the ship's course changes quickly, certain disaster awaits everyone on board. The owner and his friend rush to the actual captain of the *Titanic* and inform him of the dire situation, but the captain does nothing. The owner and his friend first implore and then demand that the captain take all necessary action consistent with common sense and good seamanship to save the vessel and the lives of all on board. Yet the captain still does nothing.

What then does the owner do? Consider these options: (1) as the owner, he can immediately remove the inadequate captain and replace him with the friend who has both the desire and ability to take the proper corrective action; or (2) in what little time he has left, the owner can pull out of his pocket a copy of *The Iceberg Prophecy*, an exciting new novel about how compelling new evidence shows that God's final judgment will occur by giant icebergs. If you and your family were passengers on the ship, which option do you want the owner to choose?

Let's look at another example: Suppose a senior flight attendant on a packed airliner flying at cruising altitude suddenly finds both the pilot and co-pilot incapacitated. On board and known to the crew is an airline pilot who flies the identical type of jet on the identical route for the same airline several times a week. Members of the crew hastily inform the passenger-pilot of the devastatingly threatening situation.

What does the pilot do? He can (1) rush to take over the controls of the plane and safely land it; or (2) pull out his briefcase and begin reading a pamphlet he recently picked up at an airport booth entitled "God's Will for Your Life in an Airline Disaster." If you and your family were passengers on the plane, which option do you want the passenger-pilot to choose?

Our ship of state (our nation) is flirting with, or perhaps hurtling toward, disaster. As Christians, our massive, intensive presence in the political process is the single curative action that can make the critical difference. We have the opportunity, ability, and assignment from God to take all necessary corrective action consistent with biblical principles and our Judeo-Christian value system. What should we do? Pray for God to bless America and . . . .?

If a brother or sister is without clothing and in need of daily food,
and one of you says to them, 'Go in peace, be warmed and be filled,'
114

and yet you do not give them what is necessary for their body, what use is that?

(James 2:15-16 NASB)

Just as the passengers are connected to the ship and to the plane, so we are also connected to public policy, civil government, and the political process—inexorably interconnected.

We are instructed in the Bible not to be "unequally yoked together to unbelievers" (2 Cor. 6:14 NKJV). This verse is frequently used when discussing the choices we make regarding marriage. Marriage decisions involve choices. Yet we are clearly yoked to our civil government with very little real choice.

With respect to civil government, we can't break the yoke unless we emigrate and change our citizenship. Then, however, we'll simply change one yoke for another. The solution is to make sure we are not unequally yoked. In other words, with our biblical principles and God-given opportunity, we must work to mold our government so that it will accomplish its God-intended role and purpose. It is the job of the church to teach that concept, but the job of the individual Christian is to proceed, whether the church is teaching it or not.

EIGHT

Good Guys Finish First

For the eyes of the LORD run to and fro throughout the whole earth, to show Himself strong on behalf of those whose heart is loyal to Him.

(2 Chron. 16:9 NKJV)

Spiritualizing Our Losses

Sadly, as Christians we have become all too comfortable with losing ground in the political, judicial, and civil arena and then "spiritualizing" the loss by saying, "God is still on His throne." Of course, that is always true. Win or lose, God is still sitting on His throne. The question we should ponder is this: Is God on our throne?

Let no one say when he is tempted, 'I am tempted by God'; for God cannot be tempted by evil, nor does He Himself tempt anyone.

(James 1:13 NKJV)

God created people and permitted them to enjoy a certain amount of autonomy. When someone lies, cheats, steals, murders, or engages in any evil, it was not God doing the evil or directing the person to commit the evil. It was never God's intent for that evil to happen in the first place.

Christians in this country have the specific charge from God to bring His created institution of civil government into alignment with His role and purpose. When we fail to do that, it is not God's failure; nor did we fail because we were under the control of God and that was His will. The negative (evil) results that occur because of our failure are not God's choice. We should not attempt to whitewash our failure by "spiritualizing" the negative consequences of our own failure as if it all inevitably comes from God. Yes, God can take a bad situation and use it for good; but this does not excuse those who brought on the bad situation, either by causing it, or failing to prevent it.

In politics we have become all too comfortable with losing due to apathy and inaction, and all too proficient in assuaging our consciences by spiritualizing the failure, as if it were some divine decree outside of our responsibility or ability to have made any difference anyway.

After an election in which those who have pledged to maintain godly standards fail to be elected and those opposed to godly standards succeed, someone will surely send out an e-mail reminding us that Jesus is still Lord. Yes, Jesus is still Lord because Jesus is always Lord.

Moreover, we need to understand that even though Jesus is Lord over all, He is not Lord *of* all. According to Jesus, He is not even Lord of all who call Him Lord (Matt. 7:21-23). He is certainly not Lord of those who reject Him (John 8:42-44). When the unrighteous prevail in civil government, we need to ask ourselves if this has occurred because countless Christians have rejected the lordship of Christ regarding their individual God-given charge to conform His institution of civil government according to His purpose.

Because there are enough professing Christians in the country to determine the outcome of the majority of the elections in this country, we can only conclude that the outcome of many elections is due to the type and degree of Christian participation (or lack thereof). The election of those who refuse to govern according to biblical principles or the Judeo-Christian value system is a failure on the part of those who abdicated their responsibility to achieve a different result. It is a direct result of the moral failure of Christians who failed to act in a manner that would provide victory.

We have become too proficient in spiritualizing failure, as if it were somehow inspirational. "What does God intend for us to learn through this loss?" we ask. My answer is simple: Don't lose again. Failure in elections comes from failing as individual Christians and nothing else, as long as the opportunity exists to have made a difference.

Of course, Jesus is still Lord and still on His throne, but elections are all about Christians yielding to His Lordship in a specific area in which many, many Christians have been grossly remiss. For Christians, elections are specifically about conforming God's ordained institution of civil government to His intended role for it in order to help protect the family and the church and carry out the Great Commission. But when the unrighteous succeed in civil government, then Christian families are damaged. As a result, the local church is harmed; and subsequently, the Great Commission is impeded. When all that happens, then our main purpose as Christians is compromised.

Christians have an assignment from God to conform civil government to His role in order to further His purpose as He provides opportunity. This means winning all possible elections. When we fail to win elections, we miss the mark, which is the scriptural definition of sin. In other words, when Christians have the opportunity and the ability to make the difference by winning elections in which godly individuals are seeking elective office, then failing to win is a sin. This is not a collective sin, but an individual one proportional to the culpability of the person. Churches should preach and teach against that sin. And remember, winning elections is about much, much more than just voting.

Farm Team Faithfulness

Christians should never be surprised when the non-Christians reject Christian values; such is the way of the world. What should grieve us is Christians behaving like the world since in the political realm that is what loses elections. Pastors and church leaders should grieve over the eternal implications of those under their care who, out of ignorance or unrepentant rebellion, ignore their Christian values when participating in the politics. It is grievous when Christians, even inadvertently, inhibit the advancement of the Great Commission and oppose God's primary purpose for government because of their wrong action or inaction in the election process.

When we think of conforming God's ordained institution of civil government to His designed role in order to achieve His intended purpose through elections, we probably think of such major political offices as senator, representative, president, and governor—and rightly so. These are very powerful offices.

On the other hand, some elective offices seem relatively innocuous. How about the office of county treasurer, or perhaps a city councilman or school board member? As long as they are honest and proficient, do we really need to worry, for instance, about whether candidates for these primarily administrative offices are pro-life? Do we measure our support by the same standards that we would apply to legislative, judicial, or executive offices?

Here are four reasons why candidates for every elective office should be measured by the same high standards of biblical principles and have a confirmed commitment to our Judeo-Christian value system:

1. *Civil government is a God-ordained institution.* For God's people to knowingly elect persons with unbiblical values as ministers (Rom. 13:3-4) at any level in God's institution of civil government is to place them in a position of responsibility and authority for which they are inherently not qualified. Eventually, they will serve as a corrupting force within the institution, out of blind ignorance, if nothing else (1 Cor. 2:14). This is an offense against God.

2. *Just like sports, the political system has a farm team system.* In other words, like sports, people participating in the political arena very often start at one level and work their way up the ladder. Often, the credentials an individual gains at one level of elective office are used to attain the next highest office, i.e. résumé building. By supporting candidates for entry-level elective offices, we are helping to position them to increase their probability of reaching higher-level offices. In these higher elective offices, we would certainly want representatives who have an unswerving commitment to biblical principles; but instead, years earlier we helped launch and position the wrong candidates by supporting them for offices where "it didn't really matter."

3. *An important part of political campaigning is endorsements.* When someone holds an elective office at any level, others running for office will often seek his or her endorsement, which provide credibility and validation. A pro-abortion elected official will have no problem endorsing another pro-abortion candidate. Electing a pro-abortion candidate to a primarily administrative office, even though no real "pro-life" issues are at stake there, still places them in position to assist other pro-abortion candidates to offices where "life" issues are affected. Similarly, when Christians endorse pro-abortion candidates at any level, it damages their Christian witness.

4. *When pro-abortion candidates are successful at any level, it encourages more pro-abortion candidates to run for office because they see that being pro-abortion is not a "deal killer" with the voter.* This also discourages pro-life candidates, because they might think that their pro-life position could be a "fatal flaw" in their campaign, so why try? The opposite is also true. When pro-abortion candidates lose, then pro-life candidates are encouraged to come forward. And the success of pro-life candidates

will most certainly encourage other pro-life candidates and discourage pro-abortion candidates. Thus, the political system tends to replicate its own kind.

Throughout this discussion, we have focused our attention on the subject of public offices. However, within the political parties, and mostly out of view from the public, there are also political party offices (Democrat, Republican, and other political party offices). As Christians, we must apply the same standards to political party offices that we would to public offices.

After all, it is within political parties that candidates are often recruited, encouraged, and partially funded. This is the arena where early support is identified, and the base level of support is engaged. Also, it is within the political party system, that political platforms are formed, promoted and often eventually become law. So it must be clearly understood that political party offices and the people in them matter greatly within the political landscape. Essentially, all of these offices are open to those Christians who want to make an impact. Christians can make a difference as long as they develop the expertise and have the commitment to get involved.

Numbers 101

Numbers (people) are important in politics. In fact, in elections only numbers count, because in an election you only count numbers. The intent, the intensity, the sentiment, the goals, the aspirations, and the spiritual insights of those who never get counted actually count for nothing. Only numbers count. That is why only when Christians are in the middle of the action with massive numbers is the opportunity there to achieve the victory that was promised in 2 Chronicles 7:14. The sin referred to in this verse which stands between us and the healing of our land (guaranteed by God) is the sin of the sedentary saint. Churches should be preaching and teaching against that sin. A "healed land" will be a place where the Christian family, church, and the Great Commission can flourish. That is why churches must establish an all-church Great Commission Citizens Corp or the equivalent within their congregation to engage all the eligible membership. Pastors can preach and teach the principles of the Political Imperative. A committee can provide the expertise, guidelines and the gateway. But in the final analysis, it must be an all-church engagement because only numbers count.

The Biblically Eligible Candidate

Since nobody is perfect, how close does a candidate need to come to the ideal standard to garner our support, or from the opposite point of view, at what point does a candidate for office become unacceptable—even as "the lesser of two evils"?

Selecting the preferred candidate to support in an election is a two-step process. First, one must determine which candidates are eligible to be considered. Then, from these eligible candidates, additional evaluation can take place which will be discussed further below. We all know that in order to be on the ballot, a candidate must first meet the basic legal qualifications, which usually consist of age and residency thresholds, and perhaps a little more. Candidates for judicial offices may additionally be required to hold a law degree.

Christians who adhere to biblical standards first and foremost, and understand God's role and purpose for civil government, will have some additional threshold standards. First, Christians must agree that anyone who thinks that abortion is a desirable, acceptable, or civilized social or public policy is unfit for public office, period. Candidates who are "pro-choice" (effectively pro-abortion) are not eligible to be considered for elective or appointive positions, whether they're public or political party offices. Second, homosexuality is always immoral, always a sin in God's view, and never to be validated, justified or accommodated. Validating homosexuality as a legitimate and acceptable lifestyle is a gateway to moral anarchy that will ultimately lead to total social mayhem. Any candidate who bows to the homosexual agenda by supporting same-sex marriage or civil unions is unfit for public or political party office, period. If Christians compromise either of these two issues, then they will ultimately compromise on any biblically-based moral issue.

Christians must only choose from eligible candidates exceeding these scriptural threshold standards both in their private life and in their public role. Pro-abortion, pro-homosexual candidates are not eligible for consideration. Moreover, the acceptable candidate will not just have a moderate, tepid position on these two critical issues, but must fully, actively, and on a priority basis be pro-life and pro-family. If that analysis leaves only one candidate in a political race, so be it – just vote for the biblically eligible candidate. If that analysis leaves no biblically eligible candidates for certain offices, so be it – just don't vote in that race. Pastors should preach that, and churches should teach that. If you have pro-abortion and/or pro-homosexual acquaintances, then invite them to church, but *don't* elect them to public office.

Our basic evaluation of political candidates should start with the mega-issues from a Christian perspective. That is why the subject continually returns to the Christian's non-negotiable pro-life position. Abortion, embryonic stem cell research schemes that involve the creation and then destruction of human life, human cloning, and euthanasia all contribute to the anti-life degradation of human worth and ruthless exploitation of those created in the image of God. With the thousands of innocent human lives being ended every day, year after year, this is certainly a mega-issue.

Many politicians (and more than we'd like to admit, many of the rest of us, for that matter) would prefer to see this controversy go away, even if it means a little compromise. Abortion, however, is a "cutting issue", in the same sense that like a perfectly sharp knife's edge, there is no middle ground. Either the unborn human is a living person, or not. Either we believe abortion wrongfully ends the life of an innocent human being, created in the image of God, or we reject that. Either we honor God by letting the Bible inform us in regard to this issue, or we reject the clear teaching of God's Word. There is no real middle ground where the politician (or the voter) can mush around.

That is why the pro-life issue serves as an effective initial screen for candidates with such clarity. There are really just two ways to take a position on this issue, and Bible believing Christians understand that. Preachers must preach and churches must teach against ever casting a vote for a candidate who will, in turn, promote, tolerate or be benign toward the pro-abortion and pro-homosexual agenda. This is true even if the candidate claims to be a Christian.

Promoting the pro-abortion agenda can be accomplished in several ways:

1. *Running for public office as a pro-choice (pro-abortion rights) candidate.*

2. *Supporting a candidate for public office who is pro-choice (pro-abortion rights).* Supporting includes endorsing, contributing to, working for, voting for, campaigning for the pro-abortion candidate, or encouraging others to do so. Supporting pro-abortion candidates also occurs when there is a failure to support pro-life candidates who oppose pro-abortion contenders.

3. *Contributing to a political party or political action committee (PAC) that, in turn, contributes to pro-abortion candidates (even if the political party or political action committee may also contribute to pro-life candidates).* Christians should only be involved in directly contributing to biblically eligible candidates. Christians should never contribute to a political party and probably never to a political action committee because you lose control over where your money will actually go. This will be discussed further in another section.

4. *Voting for a candidate who claims to be personally pro-life but as an elected official will not use his or her office to support the pro-life position for whatever reason.* What a pathetic position this is—and hopelessly pro-abortion. Always reject such candidates.

A parallel analysis of this pro-abortion checklist could be made for those advocating the pro-homosexual agenda. Many times, both the pro-abortion and pro-homosexual agenda will be promoted by the same candidate, making that person doubly unsuitable to be elected to public office and receive support in any manner, under any circumstances, by Christians. Pastors should preach that and churches should teach that.

The Pardonable Sin

Of course, being involved with abortion or homosexuality or voting to promote them, directly or indirectly, is not an unpardonable sin. But pardon for sin involves confessing the deed to God (agreeing with God that the act is a sin). Also, pardon must be coupled with repentance—that is, turning away from the sinful act. Many Christians have voted to advance the abortion or homosexual agenda, while professing to disagree with them. Christians do this when they vote for a pro-abortion or pro-homosexual candidate because the person is a friend or the candidate is "their" political party nominee, or because of pocketbook issues, or other reasons. So, for all Christians who have ever voted to advance the pro-abortion or pro-homosexual agenda (either intentionally or indirectly), forgiveness is available; but the final word is always, "Go and sin no more" (John 8:11).

Many Campaign, But Few Are Chosen

I am not perfect; you are not perfect; families are not perfect; and pastors and churches are not perfect. So don't expect to find a perfect political candidate. But you can try and should attempt to find a biblically eligible candidate for every public and political party office.

Then, only from the list of candidates who passed the mega-issue test and are determined to be biblically eligible should the Great Commission Citizen proceed to find the best one. The selection of the best candidate can be clarified by considering criteria such as the following:

1. demonstrates the personal life of a Christian yielded to the Holy Spirit;

2. understands the role and purpose of God's ordained institution of civil government;

3. demonstrates an unswerving commitment to biblical principles and Judeo-Christian values as applied to the administration of civil government at every level;

4. has demonstrated a basic understanding of the office sought and has articulated a view of the plans and programs, along with a general philosophy of governance that would be supported and advanced if elected;

5. has basic educational or work record, or other type of accomplishment that demonstrates achievement aligned with the fundamentals of the office; has some prior service record (i.e. public, church, community service record) demonstrative of person at ease with public service; and

6. exhibits appropriate personal attributes suitable for the types of public and political interface that might reasonably be contemplated for the office.

The conventional wisdom of politics sometimes is to simply look at the résumé of a political candidate as if it were a traditional job application, while not focusing enough on the candidate's personal character traits and worldview, and their relevance to the proper role of government.

College degrees, work and business history, prior public service, and other achievements, along with positions on political issues, will hopefully serve as valuable information that can tell us about many aspects of the candidate. But in the end, what the person has done will not substitute for who the person is, what they believe, and what they propose to do. The most valuable information about a candidate's background and credentials is the information that will let us know what kind of public official the candidate might become.

Two proverbs come to mind here:

Where there is no vision, the people perish . . .
(*Prov. 29:18 KJV*)

Where there is no counsel, the people fall; but in the multitude of counselors there is safety.
(*Prov. 11:14 NKJV*)

Considering these two proverbs in combination becomes a very functional guideline for examining political candidates:

1. *A vision.* Too many people aspiring to elective office want to attain the position for personal benefit, or just to climb the political ladder because they want to win the next highest office. Some candidates are like the mountain climber, wanting to prove they can do it (get elected) "just because it's there." The candidate whom the Great Commission Citizen is looking for will have a vision regarding the way government should work and how that vision is to be interpreted with respect to the office sought. It should be a vision that is consistent with and reflects God's vision (role) for civil government. Any platform or policy statements should be consistent with biblical principles and the Judeo-Christian value system, and should be in harmony with and not hostile to God's other two institutions of the family and the church.

2. *A teachable spirit.* The would-be political leader needs to demonstrate an understanding that success comes from being surrounded by wise counsel and foremost, desires to be accountable. Additionally, the candidate may re-

quire advice from those who possess specific skills and technical expertise such as financial savvy, legal knowledge, or good communication techniques. A lot of wise counsel comes from an elected official's constituents, which means that the candidate needs to be accessible and open. The ideal official will recognize and incorporate capable counsel, not be a "know it all" and not be isolated.

The two verses from Proverbs tell us that a candidate for public office should demonstrate an unshakable confidence in a biblically based vision and set of values with respect to civil government; the humility to be approachable, teachable and accountable with respect to the responsibilities of the office; and the discernment to recognize wise counselors from false ones.

Behold, I send you out as sheep in the midst of wolves; therefore be shrewd as serpents, and innocent as doves.

(Matt. 10:16 NASB)

The Ultimate Political Alliance

When Christians stand before God, we will long to hear the words "Well done, good and faithful servant" (Matt. 25:21 NKJV) with respect to our works. Our over-arching charge is clear: advance the Great Commission. Because God created the institutions of the family, the church, and civil government to further His purpose, we most likely will have responsibilities in one or more of these institutions to advance His plan. These roles become assignments from God.

There is joy in aligning our lives to God's purpose for our lives. God has certain roles and expectations for us that will certainly affect us as individuals in the workplace, the family, the church, and civil government. Joy for the multi-tasking Christian means fulfilling our charge in all areas in which God has placed us. God has the sovereign right to allocate to us as many tasks as He chooses, for whatever time He chooses, as frequently as He chooses, and to the degree that He chooses. Conversely, we have no right to ever reject any assignment from God for any reason or circumstance.

> *So he who had received five talents came and brought five other talents, saying, 'Lord, you delivered to me five talents; look, I have gained five more talents besides them.' His lord said to him, 'Well done, good and faithful servant; you were faithful over a few things, I will make you ruler over many things. Enter into the joy of your lord.'*
>
> *(Matt. 25:20-21 NKJV)*

There Should Our Money Be Also

Christians need to contribute to political campaigns for the right candidates and the right reasons. The lack of financial contributions from Christians to good candidates for elective office has led to a situation in which donations from non-Christian sources in the campaign process are even more influential. Don't ever expect funds from non-Christian sources in the campaign process to be targeted toward Christian priorities.

Assuredly, some political action committees (PACs) support candidates who demonstrate biblical principles, but the safest way for individual Christians to contribute is by identifying biblically eligible candidates and contributing directly to those who present suitable qualifications. Never contribute to a political party; perhaps consider contributing to a PAC, if it is reputable and organized specifically to advance Great Commission Citizen goals. Nevertheless, it is best to send financial contributions directly to individual candidates.

A few Christians can afford to make contributions to political campaigns that would be substantial by any measure. But for most Christians, donating to a political campaign is not something they would ever consider. And if they did think about contributing, they would probably believe that their modest amount would never make a difference.

The Political Imperative

That is why we need massive numbers of Christians responding to the call to conform civil government to God's purpose through the election process, which should include, for most, a financial contribution. This should not be a donation that takes away from our financial contribution to our local church or our basic family budget for necessities, but a contribution from the financial resources that God has provided beyond them. Christians should first meet the needs of their own families and local churches, and then contribute to their choice of qualified candidates to help conform God's institution of civil government to His intended purpose.

Taxes are not a contribution to God's agenda. They are required payments to cover the expenses of government, both for godly and ungodly objectives, whether or not the government actions are in harmony with or hostile to God's intended role for government, or whether we agree with them or not. Legally and scripturally, we are obligated to pay taxes. Taxes do not change government; instead, they entrench government. Taxes support the political philosophy and worldview of those administrating civil government.

Taxes generally maintain the status quo. In fact, our taxes may be our involuntary contribution to bad government. But our voluntary contributions to qualified political candidates can lead to conforming government to its proper role, thereby serving as our contribution to good government. We must choose to do that.

Just imagine what would happen if one million Christian families directly contributed twenty-five dollars apiece every month to qualified political candidates. That equals to twenty five million dollars per month or three hundred million dollars per year to help elect candidates who will protect the family (and the church) by applying biblical principles and Judeo-Christian values to the administration of civil government.

Now, imagine ten million Christian families donating twenty-five dollars a month. That adds up to three billion dollars per year contributed to qualified political candidates in order to undergird God's ordained institution of civil government and bring it into harmony with the church and the family.

One might say that an additional twenty-five dollars per month from ten million Christian families would do wonders for the effectiveness of the local church. True! Give twenty-five dollars per month extra to your local church for missions, but also donate the same amount per month to help conform civil government to His purpose. Contribute this money to those candidates for public office whom you, as a Great Commission Citizen, have deemed worthy of Christian support. That is less than one dollar per day per Christian family to advance one of God's highest priorities for His people—a properly constructed and functioning civil government. A little work and a little financial contribution by a massive number of Christian families will cumulatively make a big difference.

A little sweat equity, coupled with a little financial equity, answers the prayer "God bless America." When we want something badly enough to invest ourselves in just a modestly sacrificial manner toward the solution that God has assigned us to accomplish in the first place, then we will see God-blessed results.

Whose Job Is It, Anyway?

National elections tend to be dominated by issues regarding economy, as experts tell us time and time again. To a large degree, so are state and local elections. One warning for Great Commission citizens is this: never vote your pocketbook at the expense of your Christian principles.

We may rightly surmise that since governments have such a significant impact on the economic well-being for society in general (which means individuals and families) that part of the prudent provision for our family and our church would be voting our pocketbook. No one can argue with that as a general premise, as long as it does not require compromising other clear Christian positions. For instance, we should never find ourselves supporting pro-abortion candidates in the hope of improving our financial position. We cannot turn our back on the unborn in hopes of receiving financial gain. Voting to trade a few dollars for the life of an innocent unborn baby puts us in the same class as an abortion provider. Nobody needs this sin on his or her record. If you think that is overstating what actually happens, please re-read the topic in this book entitled "The Greater Sin."

Remember, for every good and desirable goal, there is a way to achieve that goal that does not require the compromise of essential values and principles. God does not act in contradictory ways; indeed, He is not the author of confusion. Nor does He lead us to act in scripturally contradictory ways, or approve of us doing so.

Whose job is it to provide assurance that our basic needs will be met, and whose job is it to protect innocent human life? The prayer found in the sixth chapter of Matthew is commonly known as the Lord's Prayer, and is alternatively known as the Disciples' Prayer since Jesus was teaching His disciples how to pray. In verse 11, Jesus instructs, "Give us this day our daily bread" (Matt. 6:11 NKJV). This verse indicates that, for followers of Christ, God has a role in getting our basic needs met; that is the reason Jesus instructed us to invoke God's intervention regarding our basic needs.

This is underscored by Jesus' additional teaching from the same chapter:

> *Therefore I say to you, do not worry about your life, what you will eat or what you will drink; nor about your body, what you will put on. Is not life more than food and the body more than clothing? Look at the birds of the air, for they neither sow nor reap nor gather into barns; yet your heavenly Father feeds them. Are you not of more value than they?*
>
> *(Matt. 6:25-26 NKJV)*

The point is clear. God accepts the responsibility for ensuring that our basic needs are met if we follow His commands. On the other hand, God is clear about His priority for the sanctity of innocent human life, and our responsibility to join Him in this area.

> *Deliver those who are being taken away to death,*
> *And those who are staggering to slaughter,*
> *O hold them back.*
> *If you say, 'See, we did not know this,'*

Does He not consider it who weighs the hearts?
And does He not know it who keeps your soul?
And will He not render to man according to his
work?

(Prov. 24:11-12 NASB)

These six things the LORD hates,
Yes, seven are an abomination to Him:
A proud look,
A lying tongue,
Hands that shed innocent blood,
A heart that devises wicked plans,
Feet that are swift in running to evil,
A false witness who speaks lies,
And one who sows discord among brethren.

(Prov. 6:16-19 NKJV)

Cursed be he that taketh reward to slay an innocent
person. And all the people shall say, Amen.

(Deut. 27:25 KJV)

Deuteronomy 27:25 has a particular message to those who provide abortions, which include those judges and elected officials who endorse or permit abortion (or refuse to do everything in their power to stop abortion). This verse also has a message to citizens who vote for or contribute to pro-choice (pro-abortion) candidates because they are more concerned about voting their pocketbook than they are about standing on godly principles

Whose job is it to provide assurance that our basic needs will be met?

I was young and now I am old, yet I have never seen the righteous
forsaken or their children begging bread.

(Ps. 37:25 NIV)

If we "vote our pocketbook" while ignoring our obligation to promote godly standards, maybe we will do all right financially; after all there are plenty of non-Christians who are rich. But once we make that choice, we leave God's assurances behind and gamble

133

on the vagaries of the world system. Perhaps we will do okay, but we also need to heed the warning of Matthew 16:26.

Interestingly, and perhaps not surprisingly, when we think about the goodness of God, we are taught that for us as Christians, upholding godly standards invokes God's provision for our basic needs. With respect to participating in public policy, civil government, and the political process, this means that, for Christians, "voting your pocketbook" comes not from "voting your pocketbook" in the traditional secular sense, but from voting to uphold godly standards and being a Great Commission Citizen. Jesus sums it up in this passage:

> *So do not worry, saying, 'What shall we eat?' or 'What shall we drink?' or 'What shall we wear?' For the pagans run after all these things, and your heavenly Father knows that you need them. But seek first his kingdom and his righteousness, and all these things will be given to you as well.*
>
> *(Matt. 6:31-33 NIV)*

NINE

𝕭ringing 𝕴t 𝕬ll 𝕳ome

Study to shew thyself approved . . .

(2 Tim. 2:15 KJV)

Churches May (Or Not)

While incorporating all that has been previously said, there are a few governmental rules and regulations churches should keep in mind when undertaking civic activity. Even though we might not agree with them, these rules are not so onerous that they prevent us from being effective and fully allow anything discussed in this book.

First and foremost it should be clearly understood that civic nonpartisan information, training, and education in civil government, public policy, and the political process are activities fully permitted under IRS regulations for churches and other 501(c)(3) organizations. The following may be helpful:

Churches May:

✓ Engage in voter registration/education programs, provided they are nonpartisan in nature.

✓ Host forums or "candidate nights" during which local candidates are asked to respond to questions and provide campaign literature to those attending, as long as all candidates have the opportunity to participate.

✓ Preach and teach about the issues of the day and what the Bible says about the role of government and the responsibilities of Christian Citizens.

✓ Allow candidates and elected officials to speak at church services. (All candidates for the same office must be given the same opportunity, if they request it.)

✓ Educate members about pending legislation.

✓ Conduct public education activities on public interest issues.

✓ Educate candidates on public interest issues.

✓ Announce and emphasize impending elections.

✓ Distribute nonpartisan voter guides.

✓ Conduct "get out the vote" drives.

✓ Provide transportation to the polls for church members who need it, and otherwise assist members who need to vote.

✓ Teach and train about civil government, public policy, and the political process and encourage full, active participation.

Conversely, there are some things churches need to understand and avoid:

Churches May Not:

x   Endorse political candidates or specifically encourage its members to vote for, or against, a candidate.

x   Contribute or solicit contributions to support or oppose specific candidates for public office (neither money nor in-kind donations, such as free or discounted use of mailing lists, space, or office equipment).

x   Distribute materials that clearly favor any one candidate or political party.

x   Pay fees for partisan political events from church funds.

x   Allow candidates to solicit funds while speaking in church.

The above lists are meant to be indicative, not exhaustive. Much well-researched and well-documented information is available on the topic of church and political "do's and don'ts." Churches should seek and rely on qualified legal advice regarding questions on this topic.

These guidelines apply to churches and organizations classified as IRS 501(c)(3) organizations. They don't apply to individuals, including pastors. Individuals can fully engage in the political process, including endorsing, campaigning, contributing, and running for office—and should, as God leads. The church should teach that, too.

Most important, the local church is fully free to teach, train, educate, activate, motivate, and encourage activity in regard anything found in this book. Just follow the missions model as fully discussed in an earlier section.

It Is Ministry

Therefore, to one who knows the right thing to do, and does not do it, to him it is sin.

(James 4:17 NASB)

For most of us, the things we accomplish in the civic arena will be done right in our own community. It might be as simple as assisting with a voter registration effort. It could be distributing non-partisan voter information to friends, neighbors, and (with permission) in church. Joining with others in a "get out the vote" effort is always in order.

Outside the church, some will get involved in precinct activity organizing and leading general neighborhood political activity; or perhaps in targeted campaigns and elections (local, state and national). They will find this fulfilling and energizing, and God will honor it.

Some will enter the intriguing area of party politics, where party leadership is determined and party platforms are shaped, advanced, and defended. Some will write letters to the editor of the local newspaper or give talks at a local club. Some will get involved in the basic forms of lobbying elected officials from the school board to the U.S. Senate on legislation, policy, and programs. Others will use their research, computer, organizational, clerical, labor, telephone, financial, creative, or administrative skills. God bless those who simply say, "I'm available, use me." Don't forget, of course, almost everybody can contribute money. Just a little (but often) and to many different candidates.

Also remember that God calls those who serve in civil government "ministers" (Rom. 13:6 KJV). Some will be called into this special ministry of public service as an elected official.

Most of the activity you undertake will be within your own circle of influence, including your friends, family, church, neighborhood, clubs, and community. You will be working with the greatest people in the world—people just like you. However, in the process, your circle of friends and relationships will inevitably grow.

Moreover, in addition to building a civil system in which the church, family, and Great Commission can flourish, you will be able to take your Christian witness, influence, and worldview to people, situations, and institutions that desperately need it. All these things work together to make God's plan a success.

How, then, do we start? As in other areas of the Christian life, you must first pray about your Christian role and responsibility as a steward of civil government. God will begin to reveal your role when you unconditionally acknowledge that you have a specific responsibility in this area, just as you do in the other parts of your Christian life. Resist the temptation to decide in advance that "this is for someone else." Instead, ask God to remove any blind spots you might have so that you will be able to see the opportunities and open doors.

TEN

Conclusion

. . . and the government will be upon His shoulder. . .

(Isa. 9:6 NKJV)

Created For Eternity

The family, the church, and civil government were all ordained by God and created by Christ for His purposes; these institutions are so important that they were created for eternity. Designed to serve God's purpose in harmony, all three of these God-ordained institutions are required for completeness. Even though they share a unity of purpose, each one is distinctive in its construction and role.

We know precious little about what God has prepared for us in our future life— not nearly as much as we would like to know (1 Cor. 2:9). But of what little we do know, we see references to the family, church, and government.

From what we understand in the Scriptures, the family in heaven will not consist of individual family units that we have today. The Bible teaches that there will be no marrying or giving in marriage (Matt. 22:30). But the concepts of the family will still be in place: the Father, the Son, and brothers and sisters from every corner of the earth, including every nationality and every group. (Rom 8:16-17, Rev 5:9, 7:9) So the family as an institution remains, although it will be different in construction and purpose.

Jesus said, "I will build my church" (Matt. 16:18 KJV). The term "church" is a translation of the Greek word *ekklesia*, which refers to an assembly of people called together for a specific purpose. *Ekklesia* was a term applied to various kinds of groups who gathered together for various purposes in Jesus' time, so the concept He was imparting to the original hearers of this message was surely clear: He said, "I will build My church." (i. e., "I will form My *Ekklesia*.")

Those who are part of the body of Christ are members of His *ekklesia*, called to that purpose. One day the entire body, the church (*ekklesia*) , will be called to live with Him for eternity (John 14:1-3, 1 Thess. 4:15-17). The church will remain eternal, but it will be different in construction and purpose from the current myriad of local churches ordained for today's mission.

And surely we recognize that the institution of government remains after reading this passage:

> *Now when He had taken the scroll, the four living creatures and the twenty-four elders fell down before the Lamb, each having a harp, and golden bowls full of incense, which are the prayers of the saints. And they sang a new song, saying:*
>
> > *You are worthy to take the scroll,*
> > *And to open its seals; For You were slain,*
> > *And have redeemed us to God by Your blood*
> > *Out of every tribe and tongue and*
> > *people and nation, And have made*
> > *us kings and priests to our God;*
> > *And we shall reign on the earth.*
>
> *(Rev. 5:8-10 NKJV)*

Salvation is a priceless gift of God, bestowed by grace through faith in Christ, which no one deserves and no one has or could earn. The Bible also teaches that for us as Christians, there will be future rewards based on our works in this age. In more than one place, the message is that the rewards, at least partially, will be in the form of authority to govern.

The Political Imperative

And he said to him, 'Well done, good slave, because you have been faithful in a very little thing, be in authority over ten cities.'

(Luke 19:17 NASB)

We simply need to understand that there is a totality about God's plan that fully incorporates the family, church, and government. When we try to separate government from the other institutions, we become, in effect, "cafeteria Christians" who pick and choose by our own preferences or traditions, those elements of the total Christian life in which we will engage and those which we will leave behind. Remember, our rewards in heaven will be proportionate to how we have performed with respect to our assignment from the *Master*. We don't get to choose our assignments; He chooses them for us (Matt. 25:14-15).

We need to be clear here: our rewards in heaven may be in the form of the authority to govern, but they will not be based on how well we governed here in this life—unless governing is a part of our requirement from God in this age. In our case, as Christians who are blessed to live in a country where citizens have the ultimate governing authority, we certainly do have an assignment from God with respect to governing. In our case, our rewards of future governance will be based in part on our response to our present obligation regarding our participation in government and our obligation to positively participate in the political process in this age. (2 Tim. 2:11-12, 1 Cor. 6:2-3, Rev. 20:4-6)

We need to fully study, explore, and understand how the creation, role, and purpose of civil government, coupled with Christian civic political activity, arise out of the totality of God's plan. We also must grasp the proper application of God's plan with respect to the way civil government supports, protects, and defends God's other two institutions of the family and the church. Moreover, we must learn the ways the family, the church, and civil government—each acting according to their God-designed role and within their God-delegated authority— then optimizes the opportunity, from a human position, for the Great Commission to flourish and excel. And, of course, we recognize that advancing the Great Commission is the single overriding charge from Christ to His followers. Indeed, the consequences are eternal for all concerned.

And Having Done All—Stand

Let's face it: anti-Christian bigotry in on the rise in our culture. No longer fringe, Christian-bashing is now fashionable within the social and political avant-garde, moving rapidly toward mainstream; arguably it may already have arrived. Even now, the secular anti-Christian dogma reflects the view that Bible-believing, pro-life Christians are a threat to everyone else's freedom and thus have no legitimate role in the political process. Already this mantra is being used to extricate Christian candidates and pro-family principles from meaningful participation and even-handed consideration in the public debate of ideas. By the time the secular anti-Christian propaganda campaign is complete, those of us who hold onto values that we consider right and basic to our belief system will be cast in the roles of dangerous, oppressive, and un-American villains.

By the grace of God, all that is happening in our society will not go unchallenged and unchecked, but what, specifically, should be our response? Getting straight to the point, Christians must get out of the pews and into the contest. Moreover, it is our obligation to do this quickly, efficiently, and effectively. Ninety-nine percent of the time that will mean getting involved in the political process on a local level. I know of no better way to begin this than through having the principles and practices preached and taught in our churches regarding obeying the political imperative, becoming a Great Commission Citizen, and establishing a church-wide Great Commission Citizens Corp in each local church.

Our community, state, and nation need involved Christian leaders who can articulate strong, clear positions. Yet we must do so in such a way that it does not reflect a mean-spirited attitude toward those who will inevitably disagree. Our Christian instruction must include not only the techniques, but also the tone and temperament required to advance our Christian principles in a skeptical and sometimes hostile environment.

The human race has a moral and spiritual dimension that many try to deny or ignore, especially in the area of civil government; but to do so will prove to be folly of great cost. Free nations need a moral foundation rooted in God's truth to survive and thrive. The other choices are decline, anarchy or oppression. Ultimately, the issue is whether or not we can face the real truth about what it takes to build a society that is free, fair, healthy, and wholesome, and that positively builds upon our past.

If nothing else, as Christians we must appropriately recognize and communicate that government is not supreme and can't be a substitute for God; we do have a proper duty to get that message out. But just as surely, we must understand that since government is from God, it is not the enemy. God is resident within the institution of civil government. He is just awaiting His people to join Him.

Because Christian participation in civil government involves a God-ordained institution established for a God-designed role relating to God's central purpose, then it is certainly the role of the church, especially Christian pastors and leaders, to engage themselves in this area. Who else is going to make sure the rest of us get it right?

Only the church can counter the massive, pervasive, unapologetic anti-biblical secular bias and influence in the news media, entertainment industry, education establishment, and other stalwart institutions of the secular society. Only Christ-honoring, Bible-believing churches directed from the top by their pastors and leaders and committed to this purpose can accomplish what is required. The good news is that when the church moves out into this area, the gates of hell (and the hate of hell) will not be able to prevail against it.

In some ways, the Christian influence within our culture and civil government is analogous to a gyroscope. With a gyroscope there may be wobbling, but when it is launched upright it has a compelling propensity to remain upright. The same is true regarding a strong Christian presence in an imperfect society.

In an unhindered, ideal environment, the effect of the gyroscope remains strong. But in the real environment, friction and the downward force of gravity begin to have their effect on the device's performance. What happens when the gyroscope begins to slow? Eventually the righting force of the gyroscope will succumb to the negative influences of the downward pull of gravity and the depleting drag of friction. The only solution is a continual input of new energy into the system.

Similarly, Christians must provide the continual force of their positive presence in the process of government to be that ongoing uprighting force that prevents the whole system from crashing down. Being this continual, positive, forceful biblically-oriented presence is the role of Great Commission Citizens, and is our assignment from God. God designed us and assigned us to be a gyroscope— continuously pointing to Him. The effect of the world on Christians is to wear them down, depleting their energy and their proficiency. Staying close to God keeps us fresh and functioning properly. That is why Christian's participation in the political process must start with and then maintain a strong connection with a supporting church, the Bible, and Christian friends.

> *Wherefore take unto you the whole armour of God, that ye may be able to withstand in the evil day, and having done all, to stand.*
>
> *(Eph. 6:13 KJV)*

Here Am I. Send Me!

Christians in the culture must be known not only in regard to those things we stand for, but also those things we stand against— not only regarding what we stand for but those things we absolutely won't stand for. Inside our Christian churches we are very good at standing for that which is right; but we are tentative sometimes in regard to those things that we actually take a stand against, especially if taking a stand means getting out of the church and into the fray. Yet, when it comes to government and politics, there are Christians who are called to do that. In fact, they actually *want* to do that.

Everyone has heard stories about people who resist God's call to the ministry because of their fear that God will call them to be missionaries in some faraway, remote corner of the earth. After they enter the ministry, they eventually understand that if God has called them to be foreign missionaries, it will no longer be the dread of their minds, but the desire of their hearts. Likewise, some Christians may feel highly uncomfortable at the thought of getting involved in the political process, while others just seem to be drawn to it. Others have yet to be awakened to it, but that awakening can come with the preaching, teaching, validation, and encouragement from their local churches.

Yet these willing potential workers lack validation from their churches that this is a legitimate part of the Christian life and work. Moreover, they are not equipped by their churches to address the special spiritual challenges they will face in this environment. Some churches may occasionally encourage registering to vote and voting, but as a practical matter, churches essentially never focus on political involvement as a critical, essential Christian ministry. The result is that sometimes Christians get involved in the world of public policy, civil government, and the political process without the whole armor of God because they have entered the system through secular doors, armed with only secular tools and training. Christians should be entering this phase of their Christian life and work through Christian gateways, but sadly the local church is not providing them.

The missions model, which features a Christian citizenship committee in each local church, is designed and structured to be a focal point and gateway for Christians motivated to accept the responsibility to become informed and involved in this increasingly crucial component of the Christian life. That is the vision.

Success will never mean pleasing all the people all the time, but success is rooted in consistency. Being clear and bold, and not giving any hint or hope of compromising our convictions, will set the stage for achievement. By conducting our political, professional, and personal lives according to the highest standards, and insisting that those close to us also meet those standards, we will build the framework for the successful implementation of our vision.

> *Then I heard the voice of the Lord, saying, 'Whom shall I send, and who will go for Us?' Then I said, ' Here am I. Send me!*

(Isa. 6:8 NASB)

Inheritance

"I'm glad I'm not raising children today." That statement, or something similar to it, is frequently heard from parents of adult children. It is a direct commentary on the general degradation of the culture in which we are all immersed and its corresponding negative threat to the Christian family.

The problem is that such a statement is also an indirect critique of the church. It is an acknowledgment that the Christian community is not overcoming the world, as well as an assessment that the world seems to be winning the cultural battle. It is simply another way of saying that the Great Commission seems to be in remission. Why else would the term "post-Christian America" even exist?

The Bible says a great deal on the subject of inheritance. We are responsible for the stewardship of the good inheritance we receive, along with the one we leave to future generations. God blesses people by and through the means of inheritance.

> *A good man leaves an inheritance to his children's children,*
> *But the wealth of the sinner is stored up for the righteous.*

(Prov. 13:22 NKJV)

Sometimes it is hard to fully internalize the impact of the multitude of incremental changes in the culture that takes place on a continual basis, but thinking about the "state of the nation," which is passed from generation to generation, serves as a marker. How are things compared to a generation or two ago? In many ways, we are much better off in the fields of medicine, transportation, communication, computers, etc. Those involved in developing these areas have done a remarkable job.

The Political Imperative

In our economy we talk about "bread and butter" issues. As Christians we need to talk about "salt and light" issues (Matt. 5:13-14) because our single overriding concern should be advancing the Great Commission. When we look at the Christian church today, we must ask ourselves these two questions:

1. LIGHT: Is the church growing externally? Is the evangelical effort of the Christian church in America as effective as past generations? Considering various factors, such as a huge increase in the general population, significant population shifts to the cities and suburbs, and a great number of Christians moving from church to church, is the percentage of the total population that are truly committed Christians higher or lower than it was a generation or two ago?

2. SALT: Is the church growing internally? Are the teaching, training, and maturing components of the Christian church as effective as past generations? Is there a material difference between the "churched" and the "unchurched" with respect to how they participate in, and negotiate, the pitfalls of the secular culture? Are the Christians transforming the culture, or are the Christians conforming to the secular culture?

If we are living in a post-Christian America, this means that those responsible for advancing the Great Commission (all Christians) have not seen the success for which many (although far too few) have worked, struggled, prayed, and sacrificed—and, I might also add, innovated. Certainly many have said that we will not let the culture drift (or rush) into a post-Christian era without challenging the traditions and paradigms of the last generation's church model. Pastors and churches have over the last several years been examining and testing new models and new approaches.

But, by and large, the one factor that the most traditional church model and the most innovative church model have both kept sacrosanct is the two-legged stool concept for the Christian life and work: church and family. There is no real place in the church for God's third institution of civil government as a core component of what He intended for Christians to use to accomplish His purpose within this nation and their Christian walk.

Christian participation in the political process might be a minor sideline issue at best in some local churches. But it is even much less than that in most churches.

Before we, as Christ's *ekklesia*, shift further and further into a minor role in a hostile secular society, we need to overcome the final barrier within the church. To accomplish this feat, we need to challenge the assumption of our two-institution model by examining and engaging in a robust, unqualified test of a biblically-based three-institution model for the Christian life and work. We preach and teach putting on the whole armor of God (Eph. 6:11), but then we fail to send out the whole army of God.

Pastors and church leaders might point out that they would love for the "whole army" to be fully engaged, and they do spend a great deal of time and effort devising strategies to accomplish just that. But we need to be sure, as a local church, that we are helping individuals find *their calling from God*, not *our calling for them*.

Mark 13:34 says that the Master "gave authority to his servants, and to every man his work". Some have an assignment from the Master in the area of public policy, civil government and the political process (along with His authority to pursue that assignment). These workers are part of the "whole army", i.e. every Christian pursuing that to which he was called by the Master. However when the church fails to recognize, accommodate, provide for or send out the workers in this area, then the church is failing to field the "whole army of God".

We need to recognize that in the three-institution model (family, church, and civil government), an individual's calling may be primarily focused on the third institution— the domain of civil government. In a country such as ours, all adult Christians have a significant role, and for some, being engaged in this process is the main part of their Christian calling. That means these Christians are involved in civil government not for political reasons, but for Great Commission purposes.

That also means local churches should be preaching and teaching the principles of the political imperative and the Great Commission Citizen, using the missions model to accomplish this purpose by identifying, encouraging, and enabling each individual Christian to excel in their calling.

Having people placed in an area of responsibility for which they were not called, and for which they are not spiritually equipped is ultimately not going to be a highly productive experience. This can happen when Christians cannot find the ministry to which they've been called to in their local church, so they just "fit in". Similarly, if people pursue the ministry to which they were called without the support of their local church, they will be going into the fray without the blessings, the training and spiritual mentoring appropriate for the task. This may produce some positive results (probably mixed results), but will never achieve God's best.

Bringing civil government into conformance with God's intended role so that it may serve God's intended purpose is a worthy calling that should be recognized, blessed, and supported by the local church. When Christians are active in their calling, they will contribute more to the total life of the local church. When it's done right, it all works together to advance the Great Commission.

Blessed is the nation whose God is the LORD,
The people He has chosen as His own inheritance.

(Ps. 33:12 NKJV)

This book offers a fresh approach to understanding the proper emphasis and role for the Bible-honoring Christian in the areas of public policy, civil government, and the political process. I pray that it will be received with the spirit and purpose for which it was intended. God bless you for reading what has been written here, but remember, it is what you do when you finish reading the book that counts.

Conclusion

We must work the works of Him who sent Me, as long as it is day; night is coming when no man can work.

(John 9:4 NASB)

Appendix A

Christian Citizenship Committee

[your church name]

1. **Purpose:** Design and implement programs that from a biblical perspective: (1) teaches the elements of Christian citizenship and the political imperative; and (2) trains, encourages, and facilitates effective individual church member involvement in civil government, public policy, and the political process as Great Commission Citizens, and establishes a church wide Great Commission Citizen Corp.

2. **Duties:**

   a. Identify or develop material and methods to communicate to the church membership, in a variety of formats, a clear understanding of the biblical basis for Christian involvement in civil government, public policy, and the political process; expedite implementation.

   b. Develop strong working knowledge of activities, both permissible and restricted, for churches under the IRS code and any other applicable laws and regulations, and assure **[your church name]** that activities will fully comply in both letter and spirit.

   c. Develop a working knowledge of opportunities to become involved in civil government, public policy, and the political process and identify "how to" strategies.

d. Develop and implement programs for training, equipping, and engaging church members.

e. Understand methods and requirements of voter registration, and conduct periodic voter registration drives at [**your church name**].

f. Understand methods and requirements for "get out the vote" (GOTV) efforts and conduct periodic GOTV initiatives at [**your church name**].

g. Develop and communicate to the membership reliable sources of data and information, such as websites, organizations, publications, voter guides, and other material suitable for church member use; provide specific information to the church body as applicable.

h. Be an effective and reliable source of timely and accurate information to the [**your church name**] membership on issues, activities, and events applicable to the committee purpose.

i. Develop within the church membership a Great Commission Citizen Corps; create and implement appropriate strategies to provide a gateway for effective participation in public policy, civil government, and the political process suitable for a variety of callings within the membership.

j. Devise strategies for cooperation and coordination with other churches and their members related to the committee purpose.

k. Prepare an annual budget for the finance committee related to the committee purpose.

l. Perform other duties related to the purpose of the committee as directed by the church.

3. **Membership, etc. (according to how your church fills committees and operates)**

The Political Imperative

The Political Imperative

CPSIA information can be obtained at www.ICGtesting.com
Printed in the USA
LVOW101859130812

294145LV00014B/164/P